WITHDRAWN

WORN, SOILED, OBSOLETE

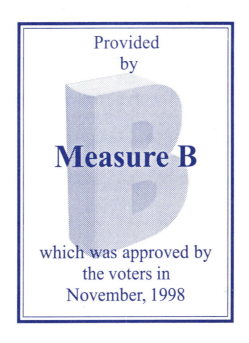

The Teapot Book

The Teapot Book

Steve Woodhead

A&C BLACK • LONDON

UNIVERSITY OF PENNSYLVANIA PRESS • PHILADELPHIA

First published in Great Britain 2005
A & C Black (Publishers) Limited
Alderman House
37 Soho Square
London W1D 3QZ
www.acblack.com

ISBN 10: 0-1736-6016-3
ISBN 13: 978-0-7136-6016-6

Published simultaneously in the USA by
University of Pennsylvania Press
4200 Pine Street, Philadelphia
Pennsylvania 19104-4011

ISBN 0-8122-3884-2

CIP catalogue records for this book are available from the British
Library and the U.S. Library of Congress.

Steve Woodhead has asserted his right under the Copyright,
Design and Patents Act, 1988, to be identified as
the author of this work.

Copyright © Steve Woodhead 2005

Cover illustration (front): Bamboo Teapot by Steve Woodhead.
Cover illustration (back): (centre): Slab-built stoneware teapots by
Sarah Dunstan, (circles left): Nestling porcelain teapots by Meira
Mathison, *Rocket Dogfish Teapot* by Richard Godfrey, Pair of flat salt-
glazed teapots by Richard Dewar. (Circles right): *Wyoming Tripod* by
Steve Hansen, Porcelain teapots by Joanna Howells, Oval teapot in
feathered copper green by Kevin de Choisy.
Frontispiece: Two-handled *Cockerel Teapot* by Steve Woodhead.

Book design by Penny and Tony Mills.
Cover design by Dorothy Moir and Sutchinda Rangsi Thompson.

A & C Black uses paper produced with elemental chlorine-free
pulp, harvested from managed sustainable forests.

Printed and bound in Singapore by Tien Wah Press Pte. Ltd

Contents

Dedication

THIS BOOK is dedicated to the memory of Mick Casson OBE, who died in 2003. His section in the book is as he reviewed it just before he passed on, and as such, I hope you will hear him speaking. His book and TV programme, *The Craft of the Potter*, started me on the pottery path, and his enthusiasm and encouragement over the years were invaluable to me. Mick loved the entire spectrum of ceramics, although his great passion was for domestic ware. His skill as a teacher, the ability to listen and give positive and constructive advice, will be greatly missed.

Most importantly, he loved and admired the potters who made the pots, and we all loved him.

Acknowledgements

I would like to thank all the potters who contributed to this book for sharing their knowledge and experience. Grateful thanks also to the many photographers who have captured the images of our teapots, making them come alive so skilfully.

I am indebted to Derek Emms whose help and assistance throughout the book was invaluable. His throwing and assembly sequence of the domestic teapot through Chapter Two is one of the cornerstones of the book, and his in-depth knowledge of making teapots underwrites the theory section. Thanks also to John Wheeldon for taking several of the action shot sequences. I would like to thank Alison Stace at A&C Black for suggesting the inclusion of a montage at the beginning of each section in Chapter Two. This turned a potentially dry subject into one that is exciting to dip into.

For checking the technical content of the book to ensure I did not miss anything obvious, special thanks go to Geoff Swindell, Derek Emms, Roger Cockram and David Frith.

Thanks to Neal French for the help and advice regarding the introduction on the history of teapots.

I would also like to thank *Ceramics Monthly* and *Pottery in Australia* for helping me to contact many of the American and Australian potters.

Introduction

Making a teapot – a potter's mountain

MOST POTTERS agree that the teapot is one of the most challenging objects to make, both from a technical and an aesthetic point of view. Creating a teapot that functions correctly requires a great deal of skill and an intimate knowledge of the form. A brief history of the teapot shows that the construction of lidded vessels in which to brew tea has been going on for some considerable time – no wonder the form and design of today's teapots are so abundant and varied.

Tea originated in China around 2,750 BC and was drunk out of small cup-like bowls. By the end of the 8th century it was enjoyed by most Chinese and had developed a reputation for its medicinal properties. At this time, tea leaves were rolled by hand, dried, ground to a powder and dropped into open pans of hot water.

During the Ming Dynasty (1368BC–1644BC), it was discovered that steeping the leaves in a lidded vessel produced a better brew, which led to the invention of the teapot. The origins of the teapot are unknown but there are several theories. One is that it evolved from an Islamic coffee pot, another from a hot water container and, finally, from early wine vessels. Perhaps these are all true. Potters began to refine the shape that was best suited to brewing tea. The earliest designs were the size of small drinking vessels and were made of porcelain or red stoneware.

China started to export these stoneware and porcelain teapots to Europe, along with the tea, in the 17th century, and soon European potters were trying to emulate the Chinese craftsmanship. The appearance of European teapots is almost entirely due to these imports from China, particularly the blue and white ware. Early examples were the Delft ware low-fired earthenware teapots produced in Holland. Of the many influences from China, Yixing arguably produced some of the finest teapots, which often imitated other materials such as bronze, sand or bamboo. In the 18th century Yixing wares were exported to Europe in large quantities, where they were held in high regard and widely recognised.

By the beginning of the 18th century, European potteries such as Meissen were making teapots in both porcelain and red stoneware, whilst in England, the Elers brothers were producing red earthenware teapots that were thrown, turned and sprigged. The English factories of Astbury, Whieldon and Wedgwood, further developed the shapes towards a more European style.

In the mid-17th century, coffee houses were flourishing in England but tea quickly became popular, particularly with the wealthy. This social change was, in the main, the driving force for the potteries to manufacture teapots. By the 18th century, the teapot had become a symbol of friendliness,

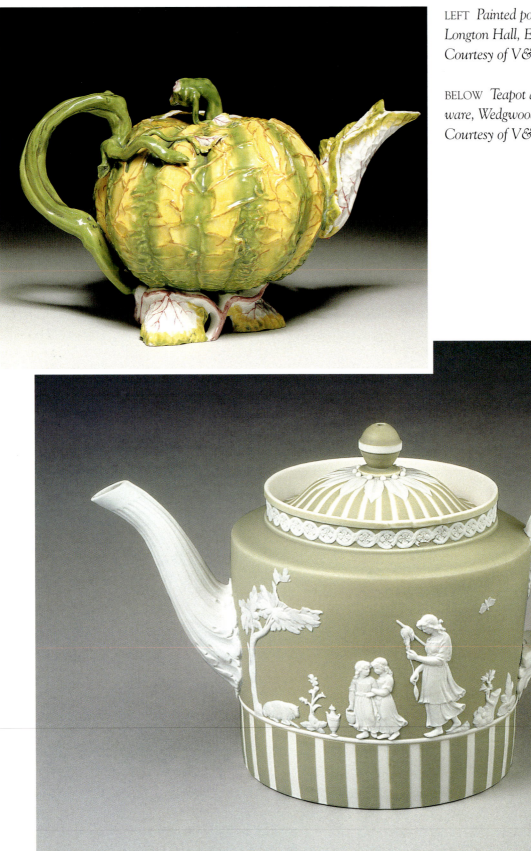

LEFT *Painted porcelain teapot, Longton Hall, English, c.1755. Courtesy of V&A Picture Library.*

BELOW *Teapot and cover, green jasper ware, Wedgwood c.1780–1800. Courtesy of V&A Picture Library.*

and was extensively used for entertaining by society ladies when holding afternoon tea parties. Later, in the 19th century, tea became the alternative stimulant to beer for the working classes.

During the days of the British Empire, cheaper tea was being imported from Ceylon and India leading to the drink becoming the popular drink of the 19th century. As a result, teapots became larger, some holding several gallons and many having two spouts!

In the 20th century, although the development of the teapot was influenced partially by the Japanese tradition, the main influences were Western.

Today the relaxing and intimate aura of tea drinking remains a universal experience. Teapots are still made in pottery factories around the world. In recent times, the teapot has been made on a more individual basis by studio potters, creating an object that is a delight to admire and hold.

I remember (with some embarrassment) the very first teapot that I made. I seemed to labour for ages making all the constituent parts and eventually cobbled it all together. The finished piece was ungainly, ugly, and useless at pouring; basically as bad as a teapot could get.

Unfortunately, there was little ceramic literature available in those days and what there was gave scant insight into the techniques required to produce a decent teapot. Nevertheless, I knew that with perseverance, sweat and tears, I would prevail.

It was on a workshop run by David and Margaret Frith that I made my first real teapot under their encouraging eye. I subsequently discovered that they had both been students of Derek Emms, who is regarded by many as Britain's leading teapot maker. Later, I came to know Derek personally and he kindly agreed to produce the series of photographs on making the standard domestic teapot.

In the chapter on potters at work, I feature a selection of studio potters whom I believe are representative of the diversity of contemporary teapot making. I have tried to capture the way of thinking of each potter, focusing on their aesthetic approach, as well as covering as many making, decorating and firing techniques as possible. I hope to show that whatever your style, you can make a teapot. Had I asked another hundred potters to contribute (and another hundred more), the chapter would still not be complete. Due to practical constraints this section has to be limited to a certain number, and so I hope you will appreciate my choice.

Teapots are now widely collected, and so the gallery of teapots from a vast range of potters should provide inspiration and delight to both potters and collectors alike. The final aim of the book is to convey the love and passion that we potters have in making them. My passion for teapots has grown over the years, and the incentive to write this book was to produce a textbook that I would have found useful all those years ago. I have calculated that the sum of all the contributors' teapot-making experience comes to over 1,500 years worth!

'English Country Garden' Teapot by Steve Woodhead.

Theory and Design

The Teapot Body

THE TEAPOT body is essentially the main component of the teapot, onto which the handle, spout, lid and foot are attached. It is also the immediate focal point on first viewing the teapot, and the main area onto which any decoration is placed.

Our standard teapot is based on a round body. In theory, for the standard domestic pot, we require a completely spherical body (with maximum volume and minimal surface area) to keep the tea hot. Practically though, this is almost impossible to make, and so we have to compromise. The aim of the body is to hold the tea and to keep the tea hot. Keeping the walls of the teapot body thin reduces the overall weight of the filled teapot and reduces the amount of heat absorbed by the body.

With this in mind, there are several basic shapes that can be considered.

Fig. 1–4

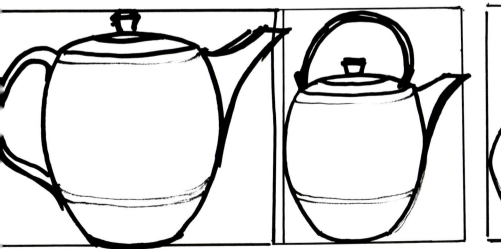

5

THE FOOT

Feet by (FROM TOP TO BOTTOM, LEFT):
Steven Hill, Petra Reynolds, Geoff Swindell, and
(FROM TOP TO BOTTOM, RIGHT):
Richard Godfrey, John Jelfs and
Steve Woodhead.

The foot creates the first impression of the teapot. It is the foundation upon which the rest of the teapot is built. A small delicate foot-ring conveys a light ethereal start, whereas a larger, more solid and bolder foot creates an image of strength and robustness. It is therefore essential that the foot matches the rest of the pot. A word of caution – when designing your teapot with a delicate foot, be careful you don't go too far and end up with an unstable form, which, when filled with tea becomes a health hazard. Always keep safety in mind!

Similarly, the lid and gallery emphasise the top of the teapot. It is therefore important that the foot and the gallery relate to each other, appearing as if they belong together.

The reason that some teapots don't 'look right' can be the result of a mismatch between the foot and the rest of the pot.

Examples of flat teapot bases
(TOP TO BOTTOM): *Mike Dodd, John Leach, Sheila Casson.*

The purpose of the foot is threefold: to keep the tea hot for as long as possible by reducing loss of heat from the surface; to guarantee stability of the teapot when full of tea; and to be smooth and well-finished, as its surface is in contact with the furniture. Unfortunately, I find all too often when looking at the base of teapots that the batt wash and sharp little bits from the kiln shelf have not been removed. It only takes about 30 seconds of cleaning with sandpaper or carborundum to rectify this.

There are basically four types of foot that can be made: a flat base, foot-ring, collar or feet.

Flat base

A flat-based teapot has no foot-ring, just the base of the teapot body. This allows the heat to escape quickly, but is popular with potters as it is stable and easy to make.

The danger here is that during the drying phase the clay may bow out, resulting in a convex base and a wobbling teapot. To prevent this, it is common to put a slight indentation into the base with the palm of the hand, creating a concave surface.

To add interest to the raw cut-clay surface on the base you can use a variety of wires:

- A double-twisted wire drawn through whilst the wheel is turning will create the classic 'shell' pattern
- Using the same double-twisted wire, but this time with the wheel stationary, the wire can be moved from side to side as it is drawn through, so creating a wave pattern
- Depending on the thickness and winding of the double wire, you can create delicate waves through to deep-textured 'ploughed fields'

For visual impact, flat-based forms usually have a bevel or moulding at the edge.

Foot-ring

The outer profile of the foot-ring is an extension of the profile of the body. This allows the curvature of the body to continue through to the base of the pot.

When constructing the foot-ring, remember that it has to structurally support the teapot during the firing process. A very small or thin-walled foot-ring may tend to warp and buckle as the clay slumps in the kiln.

Examples of a foot-ring (Derek Emms, David Frith).

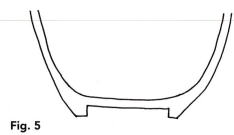

Fig. 5

Diagram of foot-ring profile.

Added foot-ring

This is really a deep foot-ring, which creates a dramatic change in form, saying 'here is the end of the pot'.

There is a whole series of different foot-ring styles that can be used here. The main feature of the added foot-ring is that it is too deep to turn and is in fact a separate piece, either thrown on or handbuilt.

Feet

Here we have a flat-based teapot, as shown above, but in this case we have added several individual feet to lift the body off the surface. The tripod foot is most common because of its stability.

Once the teapot is completed, it is the feet that it will stand on for the rest of its working life. Remember to ensure that the clay surface that touches the table is clean and smooth.

ABOVE
Teapots with feet by Mick Casson and Ruthanne Tudball.

Collar foot-rings by (TOP LEFT) *Richard Wilson and Richard Godfrey,* (MIDDLE LEFT) *Roger Cockram, and* (BOTTOM LEFT) *Joanna Howells.*

Two examples are shown here, each with three feet. However, Mick Casson's teapot has a single foot at the rear under the handle, whereas Ruthanne Tudball's is under the spout. Notice how the visual weight distribution has changed from pot to pot.

LEFT *Teapots with feet by Mick Casson (with handle to the left) and Ruthanne Tudball (handle to the right).*

BELOW *John Calver puts four feet on his teapots, but in the tripod formation.*

THE SPOUT

RIGHT *Spout by Mick Casson.*

Geoff Swindell (BELOW LEFT),
Richard Godfrey (BELOW CENTRE),
David Frith (BELOW RIGHT).

Walter Keeler (BOTTOM LEFT),
Steven Hill (BOTTOM CENTRE), *Derek
Emms* (BOTTOM RIGHT).

The aim of the spout is to provide a stream of tea that can easily be directed into the cup. What is not required is a splurge of tea that sprays everywhere. What sometimes astounds me is that many commercial teapots in restaurants and cafés pour the tea everywhere except in the teacup!

So, the aim of the game is to produce a teapot that maintains a high pressure of tea in the spout, creating a smooth stream from the end of the spout. So how do we build up this pressure?

- There must be more liquid entering the spout than leaving it. This therefore means that the base of the spout must be wider than the exit.
- The holes in the sieve must be capable of delivering more tea into the spout than exiting the spout. The holes need to be large enough to avoid blocking up with tea leaves.
- The spout must taper to maintain the pressure.
- Short spouts require the addition of a small pipe shape for directional pouring.

Thus we arrive at the theoretical shape of the ideal teapot spout – see Fig. 6 below.

The end of the spout is often cut at an angle (A to B in Fig. 7), creating a lower lip over which the liquid pours. Without this cut, the upper half would create drag and interrupt the flow.

Fig. 7 Cutting the spout.

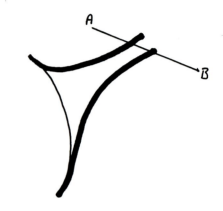

These facts are fundamental to any spout design.

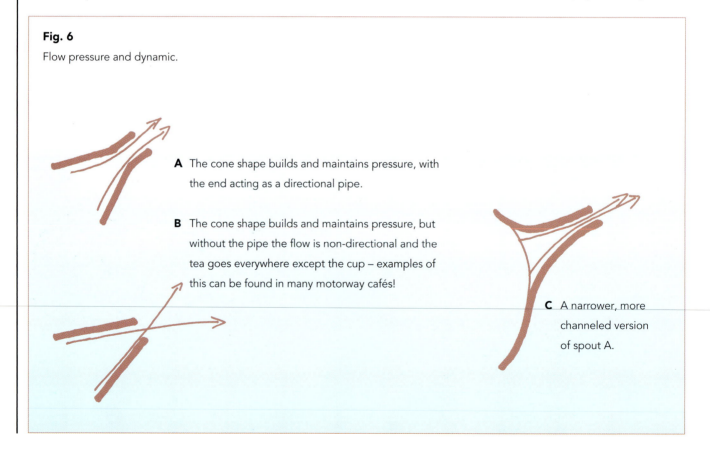

Fig. 6

Flow pressure and dynamic.

A The cone shape builds and maintains pressure, with the end acting as a directional pipe.

B The cone shape builds and maintains pressure, but without the pipe the flow is non-directional and the tea goes everywhere except the cup – examples of this can be found in many motorway cafés!

C A narrower, more channeled version of spout A.

Placement of the spout

Fig. 8

Placing the spout on the teapot in relation to the gallery/lid.

A The end of the spout is below that of the lid/gallery. If the teapot is filled to capacity then hot tea will start pouring out of the spout before the teapot is full.

B The end of the spout is above the lid/gallery, i.e. the spout is too long. When the teapot is tilted to pour the tea, the liquid emerges from the lid rather than the spout.

C The spout is at the same level as the lid/gallery (or just a fraction higher). A good rule of thumb here is that there should be a horizontal line between spout and lid.

Wheel-thrown spout

The majority of domestic teapots have a wheel-thrown spout. They are quick to make and easy to apply. Examples of wheel-thrown spouts are to be seen in the work of Derek Emms, David Frith, John Jelfs, Steven Hill and Cathi Jefferson.

However, there is one aspect of a wheel-thrown spout that could potentially make you pull your hair out – the spout twists during vitrification. The more the clay is vitrified, the more twisting will occur, i.e., porcelain twists more than stoneware which twists more than earthenware! The spout will twist in the kiln in the opposite direction to the way in which the wheel was spinning. Therefore, if thrown anti-clockwise, the spout will twist in a clockwise direction during firing.

Think of the clay particles as small springs, which, during the squeezing and 'collaring in' process, you have compressed to half their original size. During the firing, this tension within the springs is released and they revert to their normal size. In practice, this means that they have pushed the spout in a clockwise direction.

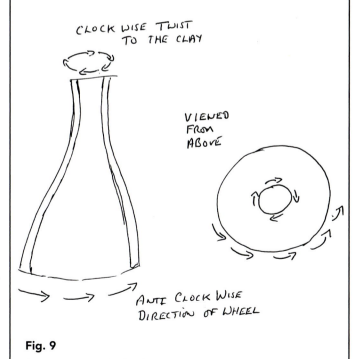

Fig. 9

Creating tension in the thrown spout.

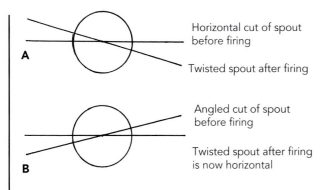

A

Horizontal cut of spout
before firing

Twisted spout after firing

Angled cut of spout
before firing

Twisted spout after firing
is now horizontal

B

Fig.10

Twisting spout – viewed from above.

Therefore, if the spout is cut horizontally it twists out of line (Fig. 10A). However, to compensate for this, we simply cut the spout at the opposite angle (Fig. 10B). Easy, isn't it? Well not exactly! The twist is dependent on the following factors:

1 Temperature – the higher the temperature, the greater the vitrification and twist.
2 Clay body – different clay bodies tend to twist at different rates.
3 Throwing – tension produced in the spout during throwing.

However, if you throw your spouts in the same manner every time (being consistent in your type of clay and firing temperature), you should be able to calculate the twist.

Another point to consider is the size of spout to throw. Cutting the spout to fit the body and then cutting the end of the spout removes a considerable volume of clay from the thrown piece – see below.

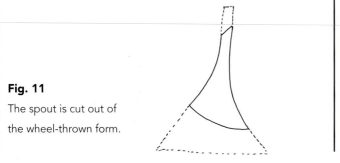

Fig. 11

The spout is cut out of
the wheel-thrown form.

Non wheel-thrown spouts

There is no doubt that wheel-thrown spouts are popular and relatively quick to make. Nevertheless, spouts can be made using a variety of techniques, e.g. press-moulded, slab-built, cast, etc. Each has its own merits and disadvantages. The key factor about these spouts is that you can create forms that you cannot throw. (Good examples of non wheel-thrown spouts may be seen in the work of Walter Keeler, Jane Hamlyn, Will Levi Marshall and Peter Meanley.)

Other methods

Just to confuse the issue, some potters, for example Ruthanne Tudball, start by throwing spouts on the wheel and finish by handbuilding them! Having cut the spout, some potters draw down the lower lip, to help prevent dripping.

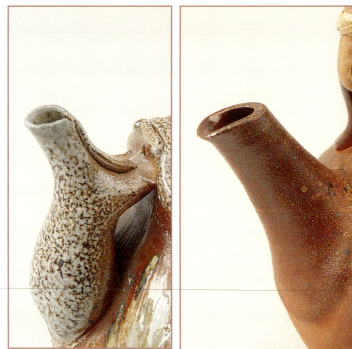

LEFT *Thrown and handbuilt spout by Ruthanne Tudball.* RIGHT *Spout lip by John Leach. The lower lip has been drawn down after cutting, to help prevent dripping.*

The sieve

The sieve has two key objectives: The first is to prevent as many of the tea leaves from leaving the teapot body as possible. (As tea bags are more commonly used these days, this is no longer very significant.) The second is to allow more tea to enter the spout barrel than to exit, which maintains the required pressure.

The holes in the sieve should be neither too small nor too large, 5 mm (³⁄₁₆ in.) is about right.

Sieve holes

Fig. 12 gives some typical examples of hole patterns in the sieve. There are others, but remember, the more holes in the sieve, the more pressure in the spout.

A A circular arrangement, starting in the centre.

B Crosshatch lines are lightly scored into the surface. Holes are then drilled at intersections and in-between.

C Crosshatch lines are lightly scored into the surface. Holes are then drilled at intersections.

Fig. 12
Typical arrangement of holes in the sieve.

ABOVE AND RIGHT *Examples of sieves by Derek Emms and Mike Dodd.*

Thinning the sieve wall

To reduce the risk of becoming blocked by glaze or tea leaves, the body can be flattened with a wooden tool at the point where the sieve is drilled, and the walls thinned with a Surform blade.

This process is optional and where the walls are very thin, some potters drill straight through (*see Fig. 13*).

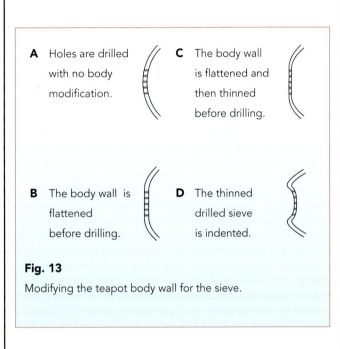

A Holes are drilled with no body modification.

C The body wall is flattened and then thinned before drilling.

B The body wall is flattened before drilling.

D The thinned drilled sieve is indented.

Fig. 13
Modifying the teapot body wall for the sieve.

OPPOSITE *Montage of handles by*
(BIG PICTURE) *David Frith,*
TOP ROW (LEFT TO RIGHT) *Joanna Howells,*
Derek Emms and Steve Woodhead.
BOTTOM ROW (LEFT TO RIGHT) *Mick Casson, Geoff*
Swindell, Richard Godfrey and John Jelfs.

THE HANDLE

The handle of any pot, irrespective of the size or form, has to be a certain size and shape to accommodate the hand.

The aim of the teapot handle is to allow the pot to be raised vertically and tilted through 45° whilst pouring the tea with confidence. However, as the teapot contains very hot liquid, there are other considerations:

- The handle should be big enough to accommodate between two and four fingers
- Provide a comfortable grip for fingers and thumb, sometimes incorporating a thumb grip
- It should be strong enough for functional use
- It should also *appear* strong enough to give the user confidence (this aspect is often overlooked)
- It must be large enough to keep the fingers away from the hot teapot body to prevent scalding (which requires a gap of only 5 mm or ³⁄₁₆ in.).
- It should flow from the pot like the arm from the body

Although many books suggest that this flowing is 'like the branch of a tree', this may give the impression that the handle should become thinner. I believe it must be of even thickness to maintain its strength. Some of the most commonly used methods for making handles are pulled; extruded or wire-cut handle; coiled; slabbed; press-moulded; slipcast; thrown; or a combination of several of the above. Examples of each method can be found throughout the book.

The handle should also be regarded as an integral part of the form and personality of the teapot, in harmony with the spout and lid. Various types of handle are listed below:

1 Side handle which is directly opposite the spout.
2 Over-the-top loop handle.
3 Two handles.
4 Side handle which is 90° to the spout.
5 Other handles.

Side handle

The side handle is probably the most popular for the traditional domestic teapot. The handle starts at the top of the teapot body, just below the gallery, and in the majority of cases springs upwards at 45° before arching downwards to rejoin the body.

Examples of side handles (ABOVE) by Derek Emms and Karen Orsillo, and (OPPOSITE) Steve Harrison and Cathi Jefferson.

Loop handle

The loop handle starts at the shoulder near the spout, and then loops over the lid, rejoining the pot at shoulder height. This style of handle can be very decorative in nature. Examples of this are found in the work of Bruce Cochrane, Steven Hill and Derek Emms (pulled); Walter Keeler and West Marshall (extruded); John Calver (wire-cut slab); Randy Johnston and Peter Beard (handbuilt); Jeremy Nichols (cast); and Steve Woodhead (coiled).

Other non-ceramic loop handles are often incorporated, as seen in the work of Ray Finch, John Leach and Mel Jacobson (cane handles); Lisa

Examples of loop handles. LEFT, TOP TO BOTTOM *David Leach, John Calver, and Steve Woodhead.* ABOVE *Joanna Howells.*

Hammond (woven willow handles); Joanna Howells and Tom Turner (metal handles); and Bridget Drakeford (mixed media – ebony and silver, *see pp.160–61*). Cane handles are very popular, and require two loops of clay to attach them securely to the body.

Leaning the loop handle forward can give an impression of forward movement. The example by Richard Dewar leans backwards because the feet have been made of unequal size. A standard loop handle would not only look out of place on the pot but it would create instability. Distorting the handle at the rear brings the teapot back into balance both visually and practically.

Cane handles and loops on teapots by John Leach and Ray Finch.

Example of forward leaning handle by David Frith
Example of balancing the loop handle, by Richard Dewar.

Two handles or 'strap' handle

A strap handle is traditionally added on larger teapots to assist in the lifting and pouring of the tea. See, for example, the 3-pint teapot pictured directly below.

It can also be used on standard sized teapots, in which case the side handle can be much smaller than usual, as it needs to accommodate only one or two fingers. The strap handle between lid and spout provides a secondary handle, as demonstrated in Mick Casson's teapot.

Two-handled teapots by (TOP) *Steve Woodhead and* (BOTTOM) *Mick Casson.*

90° handle

Example of 90° handle by Sandy Lockwood.

In this instance, the handle is thrown and attached at 90° to the spout. The pouring of the tea is controlled by twisting the wrist, which some people find awkward.

Other handles

ABOVE *Extruded coil handle by Richard Godfrey.*

LEFT *Thrown circular ring handle by Steve Woodhead.*

Profile of the handle

Cross-section

The cross-sectional profile of the handle can have a significant impact on the appearance of the teapot.

The variety of handle profiles is infinite; however, Fig. 14 shows a variety of standard cross-sections, all with roughly the same area.

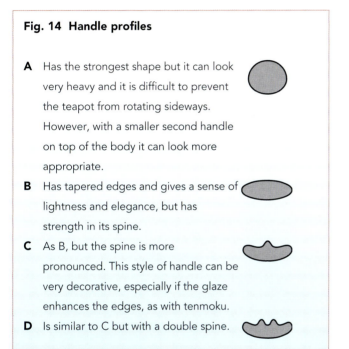

Fig. 14 Handle profiles

A Has the strongest shape but it can look very heavy and it is difficult to prevent the teapot from rotating sideways. However, with a smaller second handle on top of the body it can look more appropriate.

B Has tapered edges and gives a sense of lightness and elegance, but has strength in its spine.

C As B, but the spine is more pronounced. This style of handle can be very decorative, especially if the glaze enhances the edges, as with tenmoku.

D Is similar to C but with a double spine.

Top to bottom

The handle profile should, generally speaking, be uniform along its length. The handle is only as strong as its weakest point.

However, on a side handle there can be aesthetic merit in tapering very slightly from top to bottom. A handle that tapers substantially from top to bottom is inherently weak.

Handles which loop over often taper a little at the top of the loop, as it helps to reduce the weight and appears less heavy.

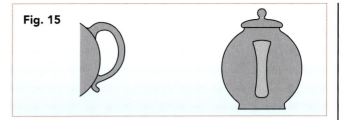

Fig. 15

Attaching the handle

This section applies to all types of handle, but for the sake of simplicity we will focus on the popular side handle.

It is imperative that both ends of the handle are securely attached to the teapot body. To ensure we achieve a strong join at the shoulder, the end of the handle is widened slightly by tapping. This increases the surface area of the join (*see Stage 2, p.53*).

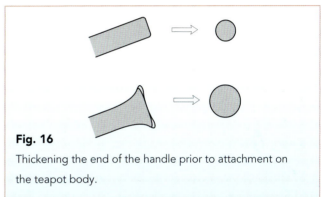

Fig. 16

Thickening the end of the handle prior to attachment on the teapot body.

This method gives a little extra clay with which to attach the handle to the teapot body. In addition, it looks aesthetically pleasing to see the strength at the top. Potters often take advantage of this intersection; some smooth and blend the two forms together, whereas others accentuate the join with thumbmarks or sprig decoration.

Attaching the base of the handle to the teapot body is just as crucial. Visually, the handle is flowing into the pot, and we can use this to create a focal point of interest, whilst at the same time creating a strong joint.

Fig. 16 illustrates a few standard methods. With all these styles, it is important to compress the clay to give a strong join.

A small wad of clay is sometimes added to the inside edge of the handle. This not only strengthens the join but also makes the space created between the handle and the teapot body more pleasing to the eye (see Fig. 18). Some handles just butt up to the body. The join can look weak and unfinished, but by adding small coils of clay it appears stronger and has more definition (see Fig. 19).

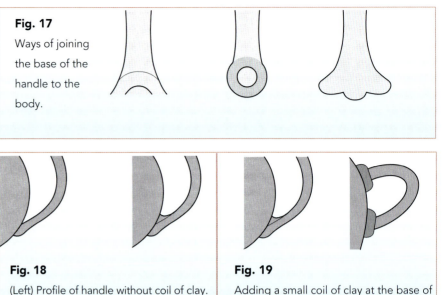

Fig. 17
Ways of joining the base of the handle to the body.

Fig. 18
(Left) Profile of handle without coil of clay.
(Right) Profile of handle with coil of clay.

Fig. 19
Adding a small coil of clay at the base of the handle.

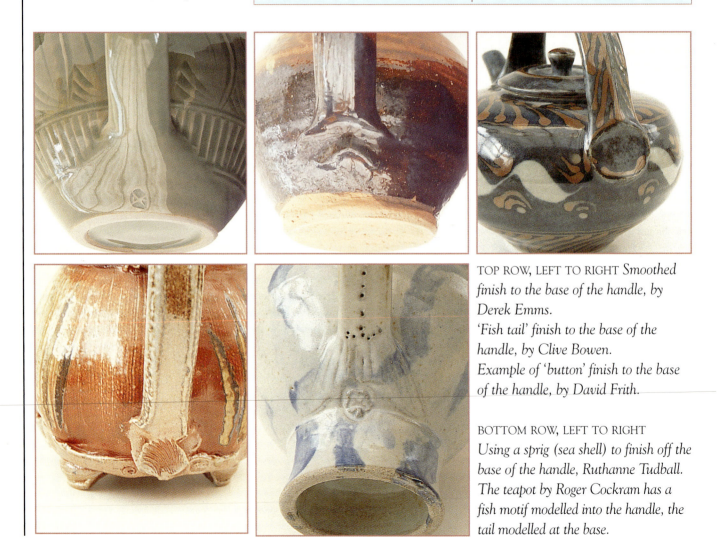

TOP ROW, LEFT TO RIGHT *Smoothed finish to the base of the handle, by Derek Emms.*
'Fish tail' finish to the base of the handle, by Clive Bowen.
Example of 'button' finish to the base of the handle, by David Frith.

BOTTOM ROW, LEFT TO RIGHT
Using a sprig (sea shell) to finish off the base of the handle, Ruthanne Tudball.
The teapot by Roger Cockram has a fish motif modelled into the handle, the tail modelled at the base.

Angle of spring

Most side handles initially spring up from the shoulder at an angle of about 45°, before curving back down to the body of the teapot. This spring is usually only 3 cm (1 in.) or so, but gives a sense of motion, tension and direction. It is important to balance this visually with the spout and lid. On a practical level, it helps to create a large enough space for the fingers, giving them a gap between them and the hot teapot surface.

Thumb grip

To help the thumb grasp the handle and give greater control when holding the pot and pouring the tea, many potters add a thumb grip. This can take several forms, ranging from a bar across the handle to a ball

of clay. The thumb grip may be the highest point on the pot, which, like the lid knob, attracts the eye. As such, it needs to be in keeping with the overall character of the piece.

TOP RIGHT *Thumb grip by Roger Cockram showing how he has incorporated it into his fish motif handle.*
ABOVE *Examples of thumb grips by David Frith, Derek Emms and Richard Dewar.*

THE LID AND GALLERY

The teapot lid is technically challenging, as it must not only be made to fit well but also add an aesthetic quality to the pot. We must therefore view the aspects of the lid and the gallery as one.

The aim of the lid is to allow entry and exit of liquid. There are several points to consider: it is important that the lid does not fall out when the teapot is at an angle greater than 45°; the lid should be robust enough to take the wear and tear of everyday use; it is important to let air in through a small hole in the lid, otherwise a vacuum is created which reduces the steady flow of liquid; the lid is an integral part of the piece and should complement the design of the gallery; and the lid should be in proportion to the teapot.

A well-fitting lid is made through careful attention to detail, and accurate measurement is vitally important. The potters throughout this book stressed this point. For each style of gallery/lid described below I have indicated exactly where to measure. The type you choose will depend on the overall design of your teapot.

'Sit-on' lid (type 1)

This is a common type of lid on a body with vertical sides (see Fig. 20). The lid has a deep flange, which keeps it in place. The walls of the gallery are slightly thickened, compressed and flattened to create a strong structure for the lid to sit on. In this instance the lid is prominent, particularly the lid rim. The lid flange is key to the final fit; Fig. 21 shows the precise points to set your callipers and exactly where to measure. It is important with this style of lid that the outer edge of the rim is slightly larger than the rim of the teapot body, overhanging a little. Without this slight overhang the lid looks weak and ill fitting.

Fig. 20
Profile of a 'sit-on' lid.

Fig. 21
Measuring points on the lid and gallery.

ABOVE *Example of a 'sit-on' lid by Sheila Casson.*
OPPOSITE PAGE *Montage of lids and galleries by* (BIG PICTURE) *Ruthanne Tudball, and* (LEFT TO RIGHT, TOP) *Derek Emms, Steve Woodhead, Geoff Swindell,* (BOTTOM) *Mick Casson, Peter Dick and Steven Hill.*

'Sit-on' lid (type 2)

This is the same lid but, in this instance, the walls of the pot are more horizontal (*see Fig. 22*). Note how the gallery edge is turned flat and is also proud of the body. Again, the lid is visually prominent, and the flange is key to the final fit; Fig. 23 shows the precise points to set your callipers and exactly where to measure.

In a slight variation on this theme, a small collar is added to form a 'neck' on the opening.

Fig. 22
Profile of a 'sit-on' lid.

Fig. 23
Measuring points on the lid and gallery.

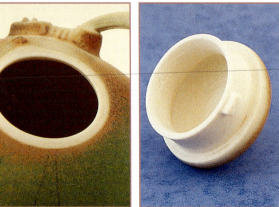

LEFT *Example of a 'sit-on' lid by Geoff Swindell.*
ABOVE *Example of a 'sit-on' lid by Walter Keeler.*

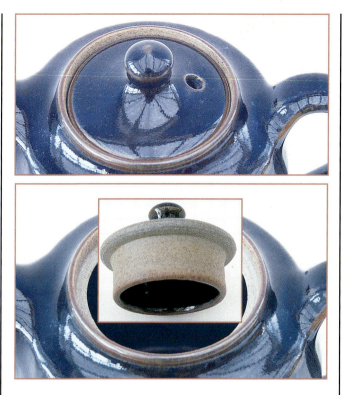

'Sit-on' lid (type 3)

Here, the gallery is the prominent feature of the teapot, not only from an aesthetic point of view but also a practical one. This lid has no real depth or locking device and requires the user to hold it when pouring (*see Fig. 24*). Having said all that, it is very popular with potters. The lid rim is key to the final fit. Fig. 25 shows the precise points to set your callipers and exactly where to measure. Note that the gallery has vertical walls.

Fig. 24
Profile of a 'sit-on' lid.

Fig. 25
Measuring points on the lid
and gallery.

In Fig. 25, the top of the walls of the gallery are vertical, however, they could be angled at roughly 45°, with the lid rim effectively fitting anywhere along this sloping gallery. This results in a gallery that can accommodate lids of slightly different sizes.

'Sit-in' lid (type 1)

This lid is the similar to the other two examples on p.28, but in this instance, the gallery is visually prominent, and rises up above the rim of the lid. However, the lid rim is key to the final fit; Fig. 27 shows the precise points to set your callipers and exactly where to measure.

Fig. 26
Profile of a 'sit-in' lid.

Fig. 27
Measuring points on the lid
and gallery.

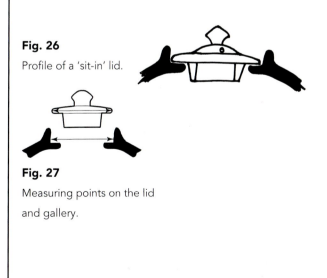

TOP LEFT *Example of a 'sit-on' lid by Mike Dodd.*
TOP RIGHT *Example of a 'sit-in' lid by John Jelfs.*

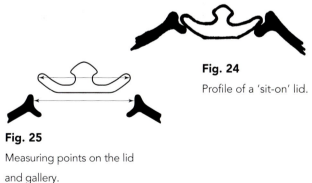

'Sit-in' lid (type 2)

This lid is similar to that in Fig. 26, but in this case the lid has been turned whilst positioned in the teapot body (*see Fig. 28*). Turning the lid, gallery and body together has created a continuously smooth flow in accordance with the curvature of the form.

This type of lid gives a very refined look to the teapot. In this instance neither the lid nor gallery is visually prominent. Fig. 29 shows the precise points to set your callipers and exactly where to measure.

Fig. 28
Profile of a 'sit-in' lid.

Fig. 29
Measuring points on the lid and gallery.

'Sit-in' lid (type 3)

This sits in the gallery rim, with the weight of the base keeping it in place (*see Fig. 30*). This lid is thrown the right way up, and care must be taken when measuring the diameter of the lid prior to bending the edges. With this type of lid, the rim and knob are the main focal points. Fig. 31 shows the precise points to set your callipers and exactly where to measure. The lid flange is key to the final fit.

Fig. 30
Profile of a 'sit-in' lid.

Fig. 31
Measuring points on the lid and gallery.

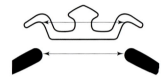

Example of a 'sit-in' lid by Derek Emms.

Example of a 'sit-in' lid by Mike Dodd.

Example of a 'sit-on' lid by David Frith.

Example of a 'sit-in' lid by John Calver.

Fig. 32

Profile of a 'sit-in' lid.

Fig. 33

Measuring points on the lid and gallery.

Another common variation with this style is where the lid sits in a sunken gallery (*see Fig. 32*). Fig. 33 shows the precise points to set your callipers and exactly where to measure.

'Cover' lid

This type of lid is used extensively on ginger jars but can also be very successful on teapots. Its key characteristics are that it sits right on top of the teapot body, and that it has no knob to the lid. The fingers grasp the lid across the diameter, so it is sometimes advisable to groove the outer edge to allow them to grip more easily. Note that the lid sits on a flattened ledge. In this instance the lid is visually dominant, because the gallery is hidden by it, and the lid rim is key to the final fit. Fig. 35 shows the precise points to set your callipers and exactly where to measure.

Fig. 34
Profile of 'cover' lid.

Fig. 35
Measuring points on the lid and gallery.

Example of a 'cover' lid by Steve Woodhead.

Lid cut from the teapot body

This style of lid is cut directly from the teapot body using a sharp knife. The cut is at about 45° so that the lid will not fall through. In the case of Richard Godfrey's pot below, he has also added two decorative circles. A small locking lug has been added to hold the lid in place.

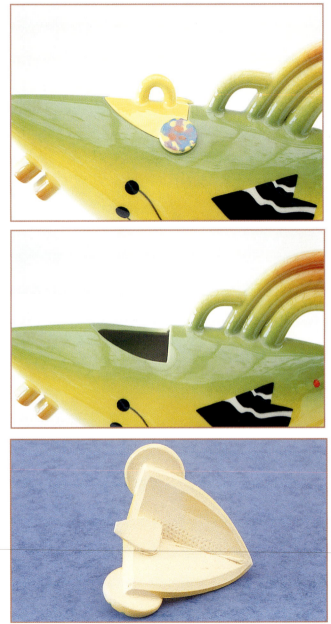

Example of a lid cut from the teapot body by Richard Godfrey.

Seating the lid on the gallery

This section discusses some of the main aspects of seating the lid on the gallery. A good fit is important, as nothing looks worse than a badly fitting lid. The key here is to keep the edge of the gallery as horizontal as possible. In the diagrams the angles have been exaggerated for illustration purposes.

Fig. 36

This shows the optimum seating of the lid onto the horizontal gallery. Practically, this is sometimes hard to achieve owing to the plastic memory of the clay.

Fig. 37

If the edge of the rim lifts during firing, this creates a gap. Even though the lid still fits the gallery, it looks awful!

Fig. 38

To compensate for the rim lifting during firing, we need to create a slight angle at the edge of the rim, so that, if the rim moves during the firing, the lid looks correct. The trick here is to use a throwing tool with a 90° edge. Using this angle, we can create the bevel on the flange and the rim in one process. *(See Throwing the Lid, Stages 2 and 3, p.43.)*

Locking lids

Lids made for other purposes, for example casseroles, boxes, ginger jars, etc, will not easily fall off. The teapot lid, however, being inclined at an angle of 45°, is more at risk of doing so. To avoid this, a locking device may be incorporated into either the lid or the gallery. Some potters regard this as a major consideration in the design of their teapots, whilst others take a more relaxed approach. Most lids can be made to lock with a simple lug or tongue of clay.

Single locking lug

TOP *Gallery by Derek Emms. Although there is no gap in the gallery, a lid with locking lug can be tucked under the rim when placed in.* BOTTOM *Lids with a typical single lug-locking device by Derek Emms. The second example has a jug-type lip.*

Double locking device

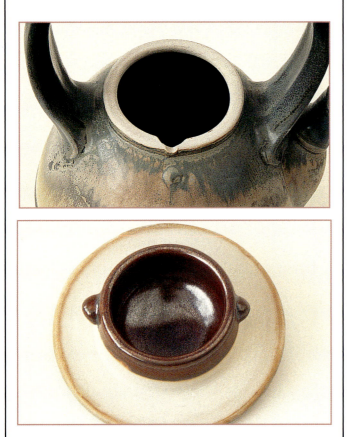

TOP *The gallery with gap cut out for locking lugs (one lug tucks under rim, and one fits through the gap as inserted), by Steven Hill.* BOTTOM *Traditional double locking device on lid by Steven Hill.*

Integral locking device

There are a whole variety of intriguing and ingenious locking devices that have been developed over the years. In the example by Ruthanne Tudball, she has pinched the gallery in at the spout and handle. The lid is then similarly distorted to make it fit the gallery.

Reproduction lids and galleries

Some teapot makers always make the gallery and lid the same size. Whilst throwing the teapot body they throw the gallery to a standard width, usually using a wooden former. Having established this, they can

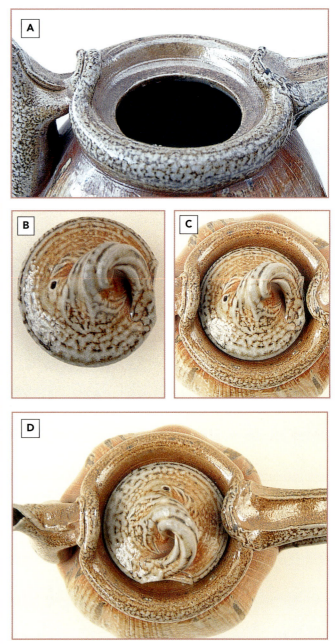

ABOVE *A) Illustrates a more unusual pinched-in gallery by Ruthanne Tudball. B) Shows the distortion on the lid, C) shows the lid about to be removed, D) shows the lid in its locked position.*

then set their callipers against the wooden template and throw the lids. Using this method they can make a dozen teapot bodies and a dozen lids and they will all fit each other. If a lid gets damaged then it can easily be replaced.

Measuring

Woodworkers have a saying, 'measure twice, cut once'. We potters should adopt this to '*measure twice, throw once*'.

The key to a well-fitted lid is accurate measurement. Start by planning ahead. Decide which type of lid you are going to make, and remind yourself of what you need to measure. An ill-fitting lid can be caused by the following:

- Inaccurate or inconsistent measurement
- Different consistencies of clay may cause the lid and gallery to shrink at different rates
- The clay may have been overworked in the throwing process, resulting in uneven shrinkage
- Careless handling: be careful when attaching the spout or handle that you don't accidentally distort the gallery. A beautiful round lid will not fit into a distorted gallery
- If the handle and spout are attached too closely to the gallery this can cause distortion during firing
- If the lid is reasonably tight but the gallery is not absolutely round then the lid will lock as it is rotated

These problems can be remedied at the various stages in manufacture:

- Take greater care at the throwing stage.
- Turn down the gallery or lid to adjust the fit.
- Sand down at biscuit. Or alternatively, grind the lid into the gallery by rotating the lid *in situ*. (Warning: biscuit dust is harmful so wear a mask.)
- If the lid jams after the final firing, then you can grind the lid into the gallery with a little carborundum paste, or use a grinding tool

The lid knob

Montage of lid knobs by A) Walter Keeler, B) Steve Woodhead, C) Roger Cockram, D) Morgen Hall, E) Chris Myers.

The aim of the lid knob is to allow the teapot lid to be picked up with a good grip, especially when hands are wet. In many instances the lid knob is the highest visual point on the pot, which many potters use as a final statement, as shown on the previous page. Where the lid knob is a decorative feature, it is sometimes referred to as a finial.

Lids without knobs

Some lids do not require a lid knob; for example, where the hand spans over the lid and picks it up at the rim. In this case, the lid must overhang the gallery for an easy grip.

TOP TO BOTTOM *Examples of lids without lid knobs by David Frith, Steve Woodhead and Petra Reynolds.*
RIGHT *Construction to support handle during firing by Jeremy Nichols.*

Firing

When firing your teapot the question is whether to fire with or without the lid. The main reason for this dilemma is that the gallery can distort during the firing, particularly with high-fired ware. During firing the clay becomes pyroplastic and starts to melt. At this point the spout and handle can distort the form, pulling the gallery into an oval. Other pyroplastic problems can occur with 'sculptural' teapots. Ray Bub sometimes supports his flamboyant teapots with clay props during the firing, and others, such as Jeremy Nichols build elaborate structures using kiln furniture.

Firing the teapot with the lid in place helps to prevent distortion. However if the distortion is excessive then the gallery will clamp the lid in a vice-like grip. If tapping the lid lightly with a stick does not release it, you will need to rethink the design of your gallery/ lid, possibly making the gallery a little thicker.

If you are firing your teapot with its lid in place then you must ensure that there is no glaze where the gallery and lid meet. Remember also that during the firing some glazes can flow and stick the lid to the gallery. To prevent the lid from sticking during firing it is vital that you clean both the gallery and the lid flange thoroughly. Many potters also use a thin layer of alumina (applied as a wash or raw) or alternatively, a wax/wax emulsion. For specialist firings such as soda, salt and ash, wadding is used to support the lids.

2 Making The Classic Teapot

THIS CHAPTER covers the making of a standard teapot – what some might call a domestic teapot. To many, this will be the key section of the book. Having defined the standard teapot, our individual interpretations and artistic expressions can take over. However, whatever type of teapot you choose to make, domestic through to sculptural, it is still important to understand the principles of making a standard domestic teapot, just as it is important to understand the skeleton and muscles of the body in figure painting. The aim of this section is to cover the throwing and assembly of the domestic teapot in detail. For the purpose of the book I am assuming the reader has basic throwing skills. There are many good books on basic throwing techniques for those that do not.

The sequence shots show Derek Emms at work; he is regarded as an expert in teapot-making in the U.K. Sequence photography by John Wheeldon.

The classic teapot that Derek will be making.

TEAPOT IN PROFILE

The standard domestic teapot we are making is a 2-pint (approximately 1 litre) teapot which contains 5–6 cups of tea, where a cup is equivalent to a standard industrial size teacup of 6 fl. oz (0.16 litre), giving approximately 3 cups to a pint. Let us now take a little time and examine this teapot in greater detail, to understand the finer points which will give us a greater insight into the piece. The pictures opposite show the various profiles of the pot. From this I have constructed a drawing of the side profile, giving the various proportions of the teapot (see below).

Key dimensions to note:

- 1:1 ratio of teapot body
- Foot-ring is the same diameter as the lid, to give equal balance
- Lid is ⅗ the width of the body

The making of the standard teapot has been divided into the following nine steps:

1 **Throwing the body**
2 **Throwing the lid**
3 **Throwing the spout**
4 **Turning the lid**
5 **Turning the foot-ring**
6 **Adding the spout**
7 **Adding the handle**
8 **Finishing the teapot**
9 **Glazing**
10 **Finished piece**

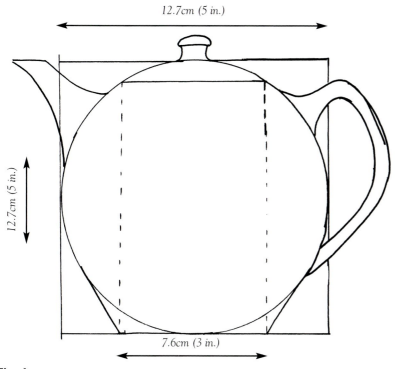

Fig. 1
Diagram of standard teapot showing proportions.

Each of these steps is a complete project in itself and I would recommend that students focus on each one individually. At the end of each step I have summarised the key points for reference, and have included all the tips and hints that the potters in Chapters Four and Five have contributed.

TEAPOT TOOLS

Let us examine the tools that we will be using to make a standard teapot:

- **Spatula knife** – general purpose knife with a thin sharp blade.
- **Metal kidney** – made from springy steel and widely available. This is used in throwing to create a smooth surface.
- **Half metal kidney** – as above, except that it has been cut in half, giving a sharp 90° angle.
- **Callipers** – used to measure the teapot body gallery, ensuring that the lid matches the diameter to give a snug fit. You can also buy callipers that measure the outside diameter at one end and the inside diameter at the other.
- **Metal throwing tool** – general throwing tool, homemade, like my own from an old hacksaw blade.
- **Turning tools** – both wire loop and blade-turning tools. These are really the potter's preference. The important point to note here is that the blade-turning tool must be

sharp. I always spend a couple of minutes sharpening the edges of the tool before a session of turning. It allows the tool to cut into the clay rather than hack at it. If the tool is blunt it will cause 'chattering'.

If the clay is a little soft, then the wire tools will cut and lift the swarf away, whereas the solid blade will tend to plough it back in.

- **Wooden stick** – whittled down piece of 7 mm (0.25 in.) doweling, used to clean out the throwing rings from the spout.
- **Piercing tool** – this is used exclusively to bore holes into the clay quickly and cleanly. However, some have a conical blade, which can easily create an oversized hole and should therefore be used with care. Alternatively a 5 mm (3/16 in.) drillbit is just as good but a little slower to use. For the novice I would recommend the drillbit as it guarantees the right-sized hole every time, although if the clay is soft it doesn't cut as well as the tapered piercer.

Tools of the trade.

1 THROWING THE BODY

This is the main part of the teapot, and its cornerstone, onto which the handle, spout, lid and foot are attached. It is the focus of the eye when initially viewing the teapot.

Our standard teapot is based on a round body. In theory, for the standard domestic teapot we require a completely spherical body (which has the maximum volume and minimal surface area) to keep the tea hot. Practically, this is almost impossible to make and so we have to compromise a little, which I shall describe as we progress. Another key factor to keep in mind is that the walls of the teapot body must be of even thickness (including the base) to even out the tension in the clay, especially when it contains hot tea.

Stage 1

Centre the clay and open out into a cylinder, leaving 2 cm (0.75 in.) of clay in the base for the foot to be turned. Compress the clay in the base to prevent 'S'-shaped cracking on the bottom. Continue to throw into a cylinder, remembering at the end of each lift to lightly compress the top edge. This keeps the clay particles tightly compressed at the edge.

When the cylinder is roughly even (7 mm/0.25 in.) width from top to bottom, then we need to start to create the gallery for the lid. Supporting the inside of the pot, press in with the right hand to create the right angle of the gallery. Note how the hands are interlocked together to give a very strong 'A' frame. It is important to create the gallery at this stage when the structure is strong. If we tried to create the gallery when the walls were thin and curved we would have great difficulty.

Stage 2

Now we start to throw out the cylinder to create the round teapot body. This is achieved during a number of lifts, preferably two or three. It is important to keep this to a minimum so that you don't tire the clay. At the end of each throwing lift remember to lightly compress the edge.

If you are using a throwing stick or stick with a sponge then be careful not to damage the gallery with the shaft! (At this point in time your attention may be focused at the base of the teapot body.)

Stage 3

As the throwing continues the top of the cylinder slowly moves through 90°. During this process the gallery moves from vertical to horizontal.

Stage 4

Sharpen the edges of the gallery using a metal tool. Note how the fingers are supporting the gallery from underneath, as well as compressing in the edge of the gallery to maintain the thickness and strength. The angle of the tool is at about 10°, so that it cuts the clay whilst at the same time slightly compressing it.

Stage 5

Remove the slurry and throwing rings from the body. Next we need to measure the gallery so that we can throw the lid to fit. Before we do this we need to remind ourselves of exactly what we are measuring. Measure the inner diameter of the gallery with a set of callipers, being careful not to damage the gallery. In addition, you could use a second pair of callipers to measure the outer diameter of the gallery. The gallery should be in the region of about 7 mm or 0.25 in.

Stage 6

Finally cut off the pot from the wheel-head using a fine steel wire, drawing the wire through whilst the pot is slowly turning on the wheel. The batt is then removed from the wheel. Whether you leave the pot on the batt to firm up or carefully lift onto a board is personal choice. You can lift the pot off the batt if you wish but I feel this always distorts the form a little.

Hints & Tips

- Compress the clay in the base to prevent 'S'-cracking
- When throwing the cylinder, compress the top edge after each lift
- Create the gallery before 'bellying' out the form
- Create a good clean edge in the gallery using a metal tool
- Cleaning off the slurry with a metal kidney allows the pot to dry out more evenly
- Determine what type of lid you are going to make and establish exactly what you need to measure for this type of lid – check this carefully

2 THROWING THE LID

Before we start throwing the lid we need to get our callipers set. Previously we measured the inside diameter of the gallery in the teapot body. We now need to transfer this to an outside measurement using a second pair of callipers. (The callipers that measure inside and outside at either end are the best.)

Fig. 2

Profile of lid and gallery.

Stage 1

Centre about 225 g (8 oz) of clay and open out in the usual manner. Make the wall of the cylinder a thick 'V'-shaped flange and compress the rim. The diameter of the cylinder is roughly that of the callipers.

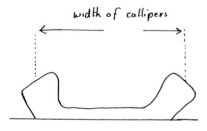

width of callipers

Fig. 1

Measuring your opened out clay roughly.

Stage 2

Supporting the rim on the inside, use your thumbnail to slit this thick 'V' flange into two parts, one making the horizontal rim of the lid and the other the vertical flange. This photograph illustrates this starting to happen. It is important to ensure the two edges created are compressed to make certain they are strong.

Stage 3

The metal throwing rib is now used to throw and tighten up the edges, both on the horizontal and vertical sides; the finger on the left hand is used to support the flange. Sharpen up the edges again, using the metal tool. Note that the collar and the rim are both angled in slightly.

Hints & Tips

- If you plan ahead and measure accurately then the lid will always fit
- Set the callipers correctly for measuring the lid diameter
- Compress the edges to give strength and avoid chipping
- When finished, double check the measurements using the callipers

Stage 4

Measure the lid against the callipers, set for the gallery in 'Throwing the Body' Stage 5. We are taking the measurement at the bottom of the flange, not at the top; this corresponds with the inside measurement of the teapot gallery.

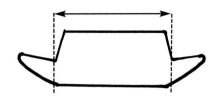

Fig. 3
Take the measurement at the bottom (lid shown upside down as thrown on wheel).

3 THROWING THE SPOUT

Stage 1

Centre 225 g (8 oz) of clay. Go right down to the wheelhead and open out the pot. Using a fast speed (because the spout is small), throw from the inside until your fingers are too big for the spout.

Fig. 4
Diagram of the teapot showing the size of thrown spout in relation to the completed spout on the teapot – it looks substantially bigger.

Stage 2

Continue to 'collar in' the spout, lifting the clay higher each time. Again, it is important to maintain a high speed during this process.

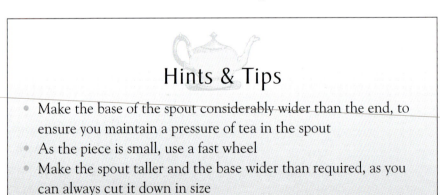

Hints & Tips

- Make the base of the spout considerably wider than the end, to ensure you maintain a pressure of tea in the spout
- As the piece is small, use a fast wheel
- Make the spout taller and the base wider than required, as you can always cut it down in size

Stage 3

Shape the spout using a metal kidney. Make the spout longer than necessary as the base and top will both be trimmed at an angle *(see Fig. 11, p.14)*.

Stage 4

Remove throwing rings from inside the spout using a small wooden tool.

4 TURNING THE LID

The seating of the lid on the teapot is a key challenge to the potter. The lid needs to fit snugly so that it does not rattle, but not so tight that it becomes stuck. Chapter One describes the variety of lids and galleries that can be used, all of which require similar treatment to the turning of the lid. In this instance, the teapot body is used as the chuck for the lid, and the body and lid are turned as one. This method ensures that the lid fits the body.

Irrespective of which lid and gallery design are used, the importance of accurate measurement becomes clear when, at the leatherhard stage, the lid is presented to the teapot body. If the lid does not fit correctly, then there are several options open to resolve this. For example, we can either modify the lid or gallery, although this can be awkward, taking twice as long. Two common modifications are as follows:

1 The gallery is impeding the flange on the lid. If this is the case, then turn away a little of the gallery, being very careful not to turn away too much.

2 The lid is too big for the gallery. If this is the case then you need to reduce the diameter of the lid. Alternatively you could turn away some of the gallery. Be very careful at this point that you do not create a weak point in the gallery structure, or affect the aesthetic quality of the piece.

Stage 1

Centre the leatherhard teapot body on the wheel-head. Place the lid on the teapot.

Stage 2

The lid is now seated in the teapot. No water or clay is used at this point, as the friction between the two smooth surfaces is sufficient to secure the lid. Using water or slip to stick the lid down creates difficulties when you try to remove the lid after turning.

Stage 3

Using the wire loop, turn away the excess clay. The left hand supports the lid when it is turned, and also creates the stable 'A' frame for the right hand. Maintaining a fast speed, turn the lid, removing small amounts of clay at a time, remembering that it is only friction keeping the lid in place. If you dig in too deep then the lid will spin in the chuck. The left hand is not only used to support the right hand in the 'A' frame but also to act as a safety net should the lid jump out of its seating!

Stage 4

Using the spade turning tool, continue to shape the lid in line with the form of the teapot. Note: at this point we have not turned or touched the teapot body with our turning tool!

Stage 5

Adding the knob to the lid. Start by scoring the lid with a tool to give a good secure joint.

Stage 6

Brush water or slip onto the serrated surface and push into this a small ball of soft clay. Using a fast wheel speed, centre the lid knob and fashion it into the finished shape. Remember at this point that the lid is still held in place by friction. The clay is at the leatherhard stage and its dampness increases the friction. If the clay becomes too dry then this method may not work.

Stage 7

Using the metal kidney, turn the final shape of the lid by moving the kidney across the lid and body joint. By doing this you can create a continuous flowing line across the body and onto the lid. The teapot body is completed at the next stage during the turning of the foot.

Stage 8

At this point, the knob is still too soft to handle, so using a small piece of clay carefully lift the lid out of its seating in the gallery.

Stage 9

Using a hole-borer, piercer or drill, make a small hole in the lid to allow steam to escape and air to enter the teapot when pouring. The small hole in the lid is crucial to ensure there is adequate pressure in the spout.

Lids without holes can create problems in pouring. For example, if your lid seats firmly and the gallery is wet, then this can create an airtight seal. As the tea is being poured, air cannot enter the teapot to replace the liquid and a back pressure (partial vacuum) is created within the teapot body which eventually prevents any more tea from pouring. To observe this, place your finger over the air hole in the lid whilst pouring.

Stage 10

To help prevent the lid from falling out of the teapot when pouring, add a small lug to the base of the lid flange. The lid now has to be placed in the gallery at an angle. To enable the user to place the lug easily, position it in line with the air hole.

Hints & Tips

- A snug fit creates the perfect fitting lid
- If the lid does not fit the gallery, remember it may be possible to adjust it after – it just takes longer
- For this type of lid use the teapot body as the chuck

5 TURNING THE FOOT-RING

When the body of the teapot is leatherhard (usually the next day), it is ready to be turned.

The first stage is to assess the pot and decide how narrow the base and how deep the foot-ring should be.

The initial throwing of the body can result in a slightly thicker base. This needs to be turned away so that:

1 The walls of the teapot body are of equal thickness.
2 The final form is aesthetically pleasing.

The next stage is to set the upturned body on the wheel-head ready for turning. Some gallery designs allow the teapot body to be placed directly on the wheel-head. However, in this case we need a chuck on the wheel. The purpose of the chuck is to hold the piece on the wheel-head whilst the pot is being turned. The key aspect here is that the chuck grips the leatherhard pot round the waist and not on the gallery, preventing damage.

Centring the pot in the chuck can be a little tricky. Some potters can simply tap the pot as it slowly spins, and it is magically centred. Other lesser mortals, including myself, have to spend a little time and patience juggling it around a bit. When it looks centred from the side, check that the base is flat by turning the wheel slowly and adjust accordingly. A chuck can be either dry, leatherhard, or biscuit; however, the dampness of the leatherhard body helps it to grip.

Stage 1

When turning with a chuck, it is important to support the piece with your left hand to add stability if the pot should come loose from the chuck. In addition, interlocking the right hand with the left provides that all-important 'A' frame. Derek is using a wire loop turning-tool to pare away the surplus clay, creating an even thickness throughout.

Stage 2

When turning the foot, the first cut starts to define the inner foot-ring.

Stage 3

Continue to turn the base from the outside to the inside.

Stage 4

Theoretically, the shape of the teapot body should be a sphere, and as such the base will also be rounded. But from a practical point of view, it is easier to have a flat base so that you are confident that the glazed area inside the foot-ring will not touch the kiln shelf during firing, and that it will stand on a level surface safely!

Stage 5

To finish the foot-ring, add a small chamfer to the outside. The chamfer (or foot-ring) at the base lifts the pot above the surface, creating a shadow that helps the eye to see the base. In addition, it also defines the line to which the teapot body will be glazed. Finally, take a ruler and place across the base to check the profile of the foot-ring. To add the final touch, run your finger over the foot-ring to round the angled edges, creating a tight smooth finish. This will ensure that the finished foot-ring will not scratch a surface when fired.

Hints & Tips

- When the clay is right, turning at the leatherhard stage is a pleasure. But turning when the clay is too firm or too soft is hard work, as you are fighting the clay
- Use sharp turning tools
- Use a chuck to protect the gallery
- Take some time to assess your leatherhard pot, the width and depth of the foot-ring to be turned
- Create a smooth tight finish to the foot-ring by smoothing the edge with your finger. This is the edge that will touch that highly-polished antique mahogany table worth a hundred times the value of the teapot!
- Make sure the base is deep enough; otherwise if it is too thin it may warp with the heat and stick to the kiln shelf

6 ADDING THE SPOUT

The spout is the real driving force behind a successful teapot.

The aim is to create a pressure of tea in the teapot sieve and funnel this towards the spout exit. Providing more tea through the sieve than can exit the spout creates a pressure, which ensures that the tea flows smoothly. The key factors to remember are:

1 If the spout is too high then the tea will leak out of the gallery before the spout.
2 If the spout is too low then the tea will pour out of the spout before the teapot is fully filled with water.

Stage 1

At this stage, the spout is still not quite leatherhard. Holding the spout in your left hand and the body in the right, bring them together, with the spout behind the body. Assess the angle and positioning of the spout visually, taking note of the parameters outlined (left).

Stage 2

Having marked the top and bottom of the spout, draw a line round indicating where to cut. Using a sharp spatula knife, cut the spout. Note that the knife is cutting both walls together, not like peeling an apple – if you cut them independently then it is more difficult to get a parallel cut. It may help to wet the blade before slicing through.

Stage 3

Stretch the spout at its top edge a little to give a more flowing profile when positioned on the body.

You may need to dip the base of the spout in water if the clay is a little dry.

Stage 4

Round the base off with the knife.

At this point the base of the spout lies flat on the bench all the way round, with the spout perpendicular to the bench. If it does not lie flat then you have cut it wrongly. If the spout is not perpendicular, then when attached to the body it will not stick out at 90°.

Stage 5

Clean out the inner surface of the spout to make an even thickness.

Stage 6

Mark off the area on the teapot body where you will attach the spout.

Stage 7

Flatten the area with a piece of wood where the spout is to be attached. While holding the pot, be very careful not to distort or damage the rim and gallery.

Stage 8

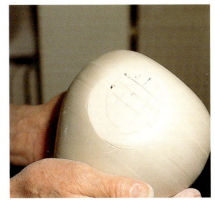

Mark the grid for the sieve with a pencil.

• Create a cross in the centre
• Add horizontal lines at 7 mm (0.25 in.) intervals from the central line
• Add vertical lines at 7 mm (0.25 in.) intervals from the central line

The final result is a grid, which is used as a guide to cut the holes.

Stage 9

Using a hole-borer, tapered piercer or a 5 mm (3/16 in.) drillbit, create holes at the grid intersections. Drilling holes when the clay is either too hard or too soft can cause problems: the perfect condition is soft leatherhard.

Stage 10

Score and slip the teapot body and spout.

Stage 11

Pushing firmly, place the spout onto the teapot body. Remember to check that the spout is extended at an angle of 90° from the pot. Weld the base of the spout firmly into the teapot body. Finally, as a design feature, you can outline the join using a wooden tool. This will aesthetically highlight the transition in form. Alternatively, you can simply smooth the join over.

Stage 12

The spout twists in the firing, so we have to cut the spout at an angle to compensate for this con-

tinuing twist. The key question is, what angle? The determining factors are:

- The type of clay
- How quickly it was thrown
- Firing temperature

Experience will give you the exact angle. However, if unsure, cut at roughly between 8 o'clock and 2 o'clock. A steel kidney is used instead of the pallet knife because it is much thinner than any blade. Tidy up the cut surface with a wet finger or sponge.

Hints & Tips

- Put as many holes as you can in the sieve
- Ensure the spout is securely joined to the teapot body
- Ensure that the spout sticks out at 90°
- Cut the spout at the correct angle, allowing for twisting in the kiln

Stage 13

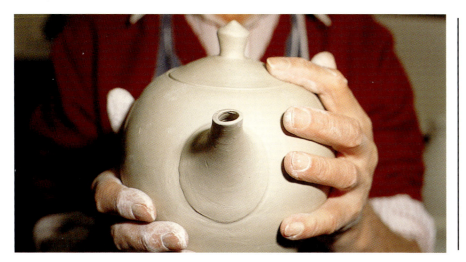

The picture shows the end-on profile of the cut spout. It is worth taking a picture of your teapot at this stage. After the firing you can assess if the spout was cut at the correct angle. Eventually you will have a picture of the angle which suits your clay, throwing and firing.

7 ADDING THE HANDLE

The handle should appear to be growing out of the teapot body, not just stuck on. To create this, we need the handle join at the shoulder of the body to be thicker and sturdier than at the base.

Stage 1

Start by pulling a few blank slugs (it's useful to have spares in case of a problem). These are strips of clay that have been semi-pulled and drawn into rough handle shapes. Leave them to firm up a little for a couple of hours. (This technique has been well covered in many books on pottery, so I would suggest you research it further if you find it particularly difficult – try *Throwing Pots* by Phil Rogers).

Stage 2

Take one of your firmed-up slugs of clay and, with your thumb, knock the end to thicken it.

Stage 3

Great care has to be taken over the positioning of the handle to ensure that it is positioned on the same line as the spout and the centre of the pot (directly opposite the spout). If the spout has not been aligned correctly at 90° to the body, it is generally noticeable at this point. Having marked the position of the handle, score the clay with a needle.

Stage 4

Mark the teapot body vertically below the area previously scored, about an inch up from the base. This gives the final position of the bottom of the handle.

Stage 5

Attach the slug of clay. It is important that you attach the handle firmly and correctly to the teapot body. While supporting the inside of the teapot body where the handle is to be attached, push on the clay slug. *Warning*: be careful not to distort the gallery at this stage.

Stage 6

Supporting the slug of clay in your left hand, join the end of the handle. It is visually important that the handle flows from the teapot body like a branch from a tree. Derek thickened the end of the handle at Stage 2 so that at this point there is sufficient clay to allow him to do this.

Stage 7

Continue luting all round the handle, including the underside. Handles that grow from the body look strong and robust, giving confidence that they will not break off. Handles that are just stuck on (with maybe a thinning at the join) look weak and vulnerable.

Stage 8

At this point we are ready to pull the handle. Full details of this technique are covered widely in other 'how to do it'

books, and I would advise students unfamiliar with the technique to practise by adding a series of handles onto an old glass jar or a large lump of clay. This way you can perfect your technique without damaging your pot. Derek is slowly pulling the handle using long strokes. The aim is to make the handle slightly thicker at the top. Position your left hand up high so that you can see what you're doing.

Stage 9

Support the pot comfortably in the left hand, allowing the handle to fall freely. Pull the handle at the same angle at which it springs from the pot. The resulting handle has a strong central spine with tapered edges, which make the handle look light but strong.

Stage 10

Having pulled the handle to the correct length and profile, it is ready to be attached to the base of the pot. You need to create a smooth vibrant curve to the handle, which is achieved in one single action. Hold the teapot body in your left hand whilst your right hand is holding the handle at the angle at which it is springing from the pot.

In one clean smooth action, swing the end of the handle round to the bottom of the teapot. The main point here is to produce a smooth flowing curve without any kinks. The area created between the teapot body and the handle is equivalent to three or four fingers width.

Stage 11

Joining the end of the handle to the base is just as important as the top join. Compressing the clay together creates a strong, solid joint.

Stage 12

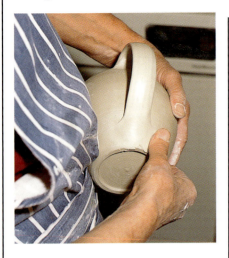

In this photo, Derek is using the classic 'fish tail' finish to the end of the handle. The decorative finish to the base is the potter's personal choice. The base of the handle must also give the impression of flowing back into the teapot body.

Making the handle flow out from the top of the teapot, sweep round and flow back into the base, gives a strong sense of completion and strength to the overall form. That feeling of strength and confidence is vital when the user picks up two pints of scalding hot tea.

Stage 13

To help the hand grip the handle more effectively, add a small thumb grip. When the handle has firmed up a little, roll a small ball of clay (7 mm/0.25 in. in diameter) in the palm of your hands. Gently position your hand as if to use the teapot, noting the

position of your thumb. Press the ball of clay at this point and smooth down one side of the ball.

Two different thumb grips can be achieved at this point, depending on whether you smooth down your button of clay at the top or bottom of it, to create a wave shape, going up or down.

Hints & Tips

- The handle must seem to grow from the shoulder of the pot
- Safety is a critical consideration and the handle must be strong enough to support the teapot when full of tea
- The space between the handle and the body must be large enough for three or four fingers with a 4 cm/1½ in. gap from the body.

Stage 14

To visually balance the thumb grip and stop the little finger from touching the hot teapot body, Derek has added another small grip inside the handle at the base.

Stage 15

Finally check that the handle, knob on the lid and spout are all aligned.

8 FINISHING THE TEAPOT

Stage 1

Placing the potter's mark on the teapot. Most potters place this at the base of the handle.

Stage 2

Review the final finished teapot, before leaving it to dry. When scrutinising the teapot at this stage, Derek is mentally reviewing all the aspects of the teapot detailed here, ensuring that all is correct. Two minutes spent here can reap great benefits after the piece has been fired. The teapot is now placed in a cool place to dry evenly and slowly. Alternatively you could use a damp cupboard or plastic bag for a day to allow all the constituent parts to settle down.

When the teapot is dry, remove the swarf from the sieve with your finger or a pottery tool. At this point it is also important to clean any other bits from the bottom of the body – being careful not to damage the gallery. Remember to also clean the inside of the teapot lid around the air hole. The teapot is now ready to be biscuit fired to 1000°C (1832°F).

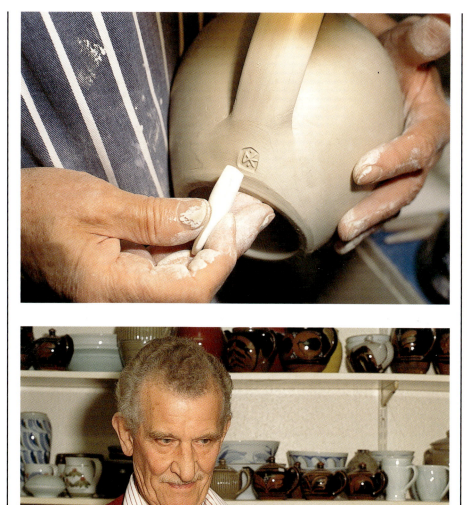

9 GLAZING

After biscuiting, check over the teapot for any bits of swarf or sharp edges – these can be removed with a piece of sandpaper. Take special notice that the angle of the spout is as it should be – a photograph of your biscuit pot is a good reference guide. If the angle is not quite right then you can at this point sand down the spout to the correct angle with some sandpaper. (If you throw consistently, then the tensions within the clay will be similar and therefore the correct angle to cut the spout will become standard for your clay, firing and throwing technique.)

Check that the lid fits the teapot gallery correctly, and that it does not jam when the lid is rotated through 180°. If jamming occurs, then firstly check that you have the right lid! Otherwise you can sand down either the lid or gallery as appropriate. (Remember the dangers of silica in the dust!) Alternatively, if the jamming is very slight, you can delicately rotate the lid continuously through 180° so that the lid and gallery grind each other down.

Stage 1

The areas of the pot that are not to be glazed can be waxed to prevent the glaze sticking to the gallery. During this process, if any wax is spilt onto the biscuited surface then it must be cleaned off, otherwise the glaze will not adhere to this area of the pot. The best way is to sand off the wax, thereby taking it back to the biscuited pot. Alternatively, you can wax the foot-ring and at Stage 6 totally immerse the teapot in the glaze.

Stage 2

The inside of this teapot is being glazed with a transparent glaze, which has a fairly thin consistency such that it will not block the sieve. Any glaze that dribbles onto the outside of the teapot can be carefully removed with a sponge. Fill just below the rim, swill round and pour out.

Stage 3

Pour the glaze out through the spout. If your glaze is very thick, you will need to blow down the spout in order to clear glaze out of the sieve.

Stage 4

With your finger over the air hole, pour the glaze into the lid, leave for roughly three seconds then pour out. Clean the edge thoroughly with a sponge.

Stage 5

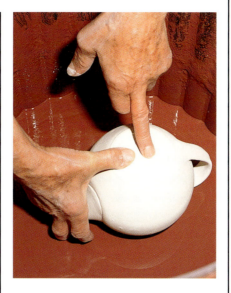

Leave the glaze to dry overnight. If the pot is damp then you will get uneven application of the tenmoku glaze. Now comes the difficult bit. When you dip the teapot into the glaze you do not want the glaze to go inside the already-glazed spout. Here the teapot is being put into the glaze upside down. The trick here is to be able to hold the teapot with finger and thumb so that the finger blocks the spout. The other hand then steadies the pot as it is immersed in the glaze. Push the pot down into the glaze up to the bevelled edge of the foot.

The alternative way that I use is to get a small piece of clay or sponge (1 x 1 x 5 cm / ⅜ x ⅜ x 2 in.) and put it into the end of the spout. This prevents glaze from entering the spout. You must remove the sponge immediately the pot is removed from the glaze.

Stage 6

Removing the teapot from the glaze. Note that the base and inside of the foot-ring are still left unglazed.

Stage 7

Hold the teapot carefully with the hand inside the gallery. Then, using a spoon, pour a little of the glaze into the foot-ring if you have one. Clean the foot-ring with a sponge to remove any surplus glaze.

Stage 8

Hold the lid by the flange and with your middle finger over the air hole, dip the lid into the glaze. Your finger will prevent the glaze from filling the inside of the lid. Once the glaze has dried, use your small drill bit or piercer and clean out the air hole in the lid, being careful not to chip the glaze too much. A little chipping will occur but this does not matter as the surface will melt smooth during the firing.

Stage 9

Clean the teapot gallery thoroughly with a sponge, ensuring that no glaze remains. Double check that the corner deep in the gallery is clean, as it is sometimes difficult to get the sponge right inside.

Stage 10

Place the teapot in the kiln and reduction fire to cone 10 (1305°C/2381°F). These are being fired with the lid in position to avoid warping.

10 FINISHED PIECE

Stage 1

After removing from the kiln, check that the piece is ok. Check that the lid fits correctly. With some sandpaper or similar, smooth the base, feet, gallery and lid.

Stage 2

The ultimate test is to tilt the teapot through 90° and confirm that the lid does not fall out. Before you do this ensure that the lid's locking device is by the handle, secondly I would advise you to perform this over a soft cushion rather than a concrete floor!

Finally we have the teapot pouring the tea. Note the beautiful stream of tea flowing from the spout!

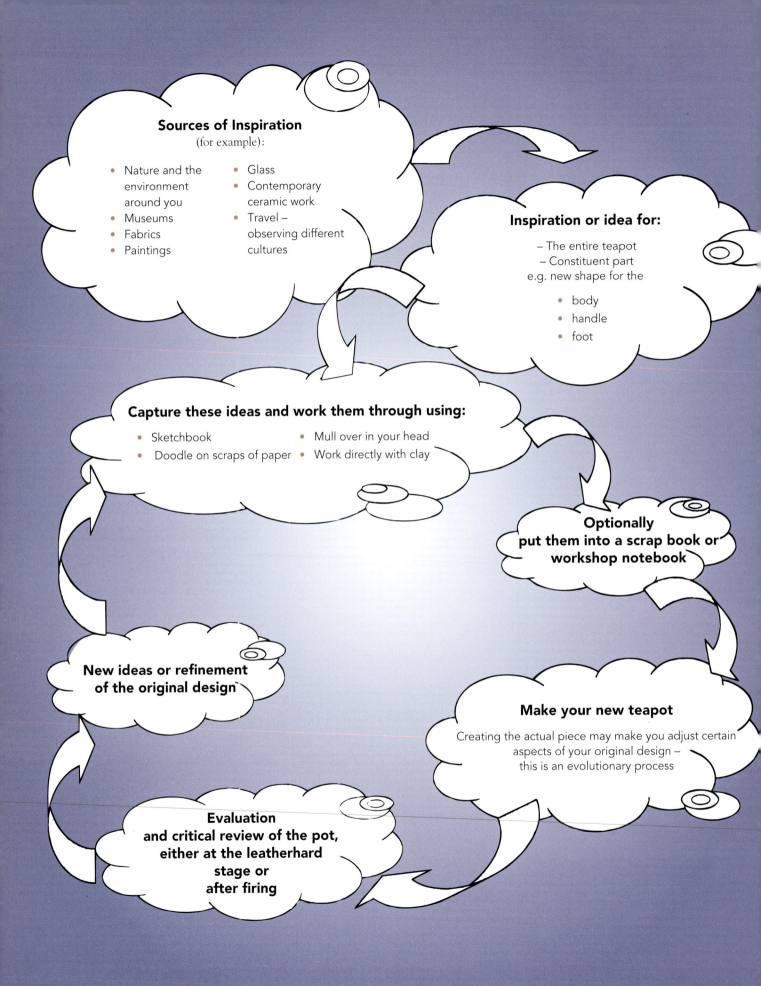

Sources of Inspiration
(for example):

- Nature and the environment around you
- Museums
- Fabrics
- Paintings
- Glass
- Contemporary ceramic work
- Travel – observing different cultures

Inspiration or idea for:

– The entire teapot
– Constituent part
e.g. new shape for the

- body
- handle
- foot

Capture these ideas and work them through using:

- Sketchbook
- Doodle on scraps of paper
- Mull over in your head
- Work directly with clay

Optionally put them into a scrap book or workshop notebook

New ideas or refinement of the original design

Make your new teapot

Creating the actual piece may make you adjust certain aspects of your original design – this is an evolutionary process

Evaluation and critical review of the pot, either at the leatherhard stage or after firing

3 Artistic Development

Introduction

CHAPTERS ONE AND TWO described the detailed steps for making a standard domestic teapot, which most potters will make at some point in their working lives.

The teapot is a magical form as it allows the potter to explore shape and decoration within extensive boundaries, and yet still be recognised as a teapot. In conjunction with this, there is a market for teapots amongst people who collect them. This demand for teapots, in all their guises, has encouraged potters to make the wide variety we see today.

Designing a new style of teapot can be a very difficult and daunting task. In Chapters Four and Five, a whole spectrum of potters describe their influences and sources of inspiration. This is an individual process, and very often reflects the lifestyle, working environment and background of the artist. It is also an iterative or cyclical process, as the design is continually being refined. As with our natural environment, our creative work evolves over time.

In order to illustrate some of the design issues to be considered, it is useful to look at the thought process and approach of various potters. While many simply work through their designs while sitting at the wheel or workbench, trying out ideas in clay as they go along and slowly evolving new pieces, others work out their ideas, (some quite specifically), through the use of sketchbooks, templates or maquettes. Every potter develops their work quite differently, and the variety of responses given here reflects this.

OPPOSITE

Fig. 1

Designing teapots – an evolutionary approach.

Richard Dewar

'As most children do, I started drawing before I discovered clay. The drawing process has stayed with me since the age of two or three and seems as natural to me as breathing. I've never stopped doing it. Whether for greeting cards, kitchen and house plans, describing a process, or simply scribbling down ideas, I draw as often as I read books, and that's quite a lot.

The fact that I am constantly drawing, designing and describing my work on paper is so much part of the making process that it has become part of my working day. The drawing book is always open on a table somewhere in the studio.'

Sarah Dunstan

'My sketchbooks are fragments of ideas that are collaged together. I do not design my work on paper beforehand, it is more of an evolving process during the making. My sketchbooks are full of drawings, paintings, photographs of places that I've been to, cuttings and postcards which I collect simply because they inspire me. Looking through my sketchbooks there are certain recurring themes of architectural details, typography, colour combinations, surface decoration and quirky domestic objects.'

Sarah Dunstan's drawing and collage book.

Richard Godfrey

'Drawing for me is an essential part of the creative process. It usually takes the form of quick sketches and notes about ideas, not only for forms and decoration but also for processes and firing techniques. I use a hardback sketchbook for outdoor trips but in the studio I mostly use plain A4 refill pads. I draw with pencil and biro and sometimes use watercolour.

Ideas for forms are often derived from things that I pick up on the beach. Shells, bits of wood, plastic bottles, in fact just about anything. I walk a great deal and usually find things in the hedgerows to inspire me. I love natural forms like insects, seeds and berries. My studio is right on the cliffs here in south Devon, in a very unspoilt area. The light is wonderful and I find a great deal of intense colour throughout the year. I enjoy the changing seasons as each brings its own beauty. The sunrises in February are often spectacular; the wild flowers in May and June create great sweeps of colour across the cliffs, the berries and bramble leaves of autumn provide intense focal points. I take a lot of photographs, both slides and prints and often use these as source material from which to draw. The drawing process for me is a way of distilling the essence of what I have seen, looking for whatever it was that touched my button, in order that I might use it to touch someone else's.'

Pages from Richard Godfrey's sketchbook.

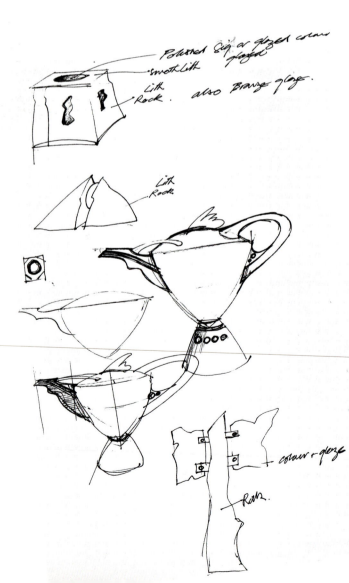

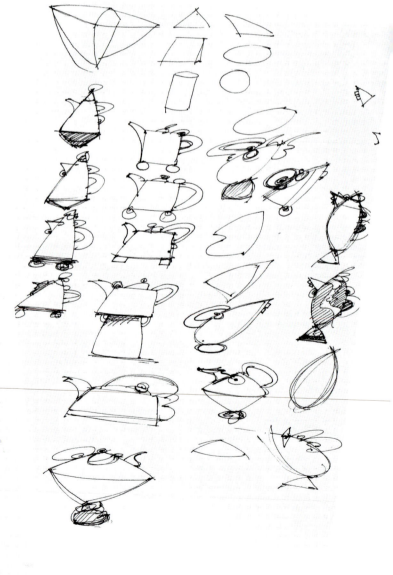

Walter Keeler

'Some of my ideas come straight from the process of making, inspired by, for example, changing a form dramatically by hitting it with the hard edge of a stick or piece of metal while the clay is leatherhard. On other occasions an idea begins rather vaguely in my head and has to be coaxed into focus, or developed by drawing in my sketchbook. In this way an initial idea may travel a long way, through various transitions before it is realised in clay. Often, even after this protracted design process, the final decisions and refinements happen in the making.

There is also a sort of cannibalisation that occurs, taking elements (such as a handle or a spout perhaps)

Four pages from Walter Keeler's sketchbook, showing the development of ideas and forms.

and using them in the context of
another pot, exploiting their potential more fully or in a different
way. All of this is fed by outside
influences; from historical pots,
metal vessels or from the natural
world, even (dare I say it) by
conceptual ideas!'

Lisa Krigel

'The sculptural teapot has developed from my fascination with the fine line between form and function. This delicate balance is to be seen in much of my source material, particularly street fashions observed around the city or in magazines. Developing new work is always an amalgam of images seen, an interesting fabric print in a magazine or an unusual handbag on the street, combined with the issues dealt with in my most recent work.

The sketchbook is always with me. It is my recorder, my memory jogger, my "what if…?" My things to do list. It is often the most substantial link between the germ of an idea and the making process.

Working within ceramics it is impossible to ignore the tradition of pottery and the production of functional ware, and it is important to realise that an obsession with form can often lead away from function. The balance is always delicate, as a development of form could compromise the function and of course any attention to function could weaken the form.'

Pages from Lisa Krigel's sketchbook.

Peter
Meanley

'I have always drawn. It is an activity which is pleasurable in itself; there is something magic about putting black lines on paper – whether the lines are an end in themselves, perhaps a drawing which is just a drawing, or for me the potter, sculptor and vessel-maker, the means of recording or developing an idea.

Drawing is a wonderful tool for me the vessel-maker. I find that I am sometimes bombarded with ideas – one after the other in the space of perhaps a few seconds. The important thing then is to get these down fast on paper – perhaps with the addition of simple notations. When I have done this I feel that the idea is safe and I can return to it whenever I wish. This may be immediately or perhaps next week or next year. The surprising thing is that I can still feel an excitement from a series of marks on paper I may have made 20 years previously, and which I might now see differently and be able to develop further.

The start of an idea is very exciting. It can be something seen; perhaps a domestic tool or

ABOVE and OPPOSITE
Drawings from Peter Meanley.

a piece of furniture; perhaps it is a series of shadows in an Elizabethan building or a Gothic cathedral. It can be almost anything. But I have to get this surge of emotion down – on paper. In my own time, later, I can examine it again, and I will draw quickly and repeatedly to try to capture the essence of the idea. Sometimes I can work it out this way and sometimes I cannot. Sometimes I have to be analytical to identify and understand the essence of the idea; those parts or proportions which must be protected at all costs. When I understand the seeds of the idea I may expand around it . . . then if the time is right, I will start to make.

My teapots or 'spouted pouring vessels' are assemblages of bits. I throw or make lots of parts; many more than I need and then I play with them. I cut them up and stick them together. The title 'spouted pouring vessels' gives me the latitude with the form. The word 'teapot' suggests a solution, but the 'spouted pouring vessel' can be almost anything. For me it has to contain and dispense liquid. It also has to be liftable and of a finite size, and of course it will be salt fired. But I don't merely reproduce what is in the sketchbook. I understand the idea and then play around with it. A big form or volume may require an appendage which is very small. The join or edge will have to be particular. I put together 3D pieces to try to make a harmony; to create an integrity within the piece being made.

When I am making, the drawing is there as a reference but not as a model. The pieces of clay are real; the idea must work through this medium – clay and salt glaze. Therefore where necessary the clay may identify problems or restrictions which the drawing could not.

There is a wonderful relationship between drawing and clay. A drawing may take 10 seconds or 5 minutes. A lot of ground can be covered very quickly. In any one session I might cover 5 or 6 pages, perhaps 30 or 40 forms – perhaps in a ½ hour session. In clay

work, time is slower. I can make perhaps 4 spouted pouring vessels (in the clay stage) in a week. The 'turnover of ideas' is much slower, therefore I try to be reasonably clear about the idea before I start.

I have made a few good pots. Unfortunately I have also made a lot which are not and some which are appalling. Afterwards I sometimes think how did I get it so wrong? But you always look forward to the next one which will be much better.'

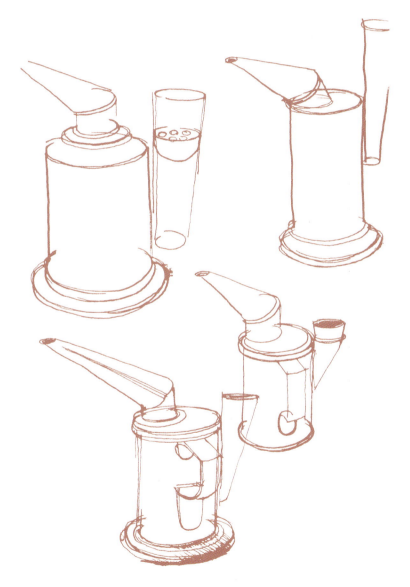

Steve Woodhead

Throughout history potters have been inspired by other potters' work, and this process still continues today. When the source piece is ancient and from a museum for example then there are no qualms about copying elements from the pot. With a more contemporary piece there is generally more reluctance.

If we take my 'Cockerel' teapot as an example, the inspiration for this teapot came from the teapot of Mick Casson (see p.100). I thought its form had such magnificent strength and vitality, full of life and humour – much like the man himself. Having been inspired, I knew that, with a few modifications, this style would suit my work very nicely.

To adapt Mick's form so that it was right for my style and glazes, I made the following modifications;

- The handles, feet and lid knob are made from coils of clay impressed with a grooved surface. This is my standard workshop practice and is designed to give a surface over which the glazes can flow
- My cockerel spout has not got the pronounced bend of Mick's spout.
- At the base of the teapot body I created a decorative finish to allow my runny glazes to pool
- To prevent the glazes flowing down onto the foot and sticking to the kiln shelf, I limit the glazing around the feet.
- The body of my pot is taller and squarer than Mick's.

I think everyone would agree that the finished teapot is heavily influenced by Mick Casson's, but is my own interpretation.

The question here is – did I copy Mick's teapot? Well yes, his form inspired me, but I think I have put sufficient of my stamp onto it to make it mine. If I made exactly the same form and salt fired it, I think I would have a harder time convincing myself of this.

So, the bottom line is, don't be afraid of creating your own teapots based on others that inspire you. This is a natural process, and as we have been making pots for thousands of years, few ideas can be entirely original!

Having got this far, I then developed the form further by putting circular handles on it. In time, other teapots will evolve from this form, and so it goes on.

Porcelain 'Cockerel' teapot, height: 22.5 cm (9 in.), by Steve Woodhead.

Bamboo Handle Teapot

Bamboo Handle Teapot, *height: 25 cm (10 in.), porcelain, by Steve Woodhead.*

The inspiration for this piece was focused on the handle. Whilst watching a TV programme on the building of office blocks in the Far East, I noticed that they used bamboo poles strapped together rather than metal scaffolding poles. This was the inspiration I needed!

Fig. 2
Design notes for *Bamboo Handle Teapot.*

1 Coil of clay 7 mm/0.25 in. in diameter, along which I create a spiral groove using a wooden stick.

2 Taking three of these coils I strap them together, adding a small button to help strengthen them. I then lay this over a curved surface to stiffen up. Finally I add a smaller coil, but lift the ends to give a spring to the handle.

3 With this complete I can then use four coils to create two 'A' frames for mounting the handle.

4 My initial intention was to put this new handle on the 'Oriental' teapot. However, on reviewing this, I thought the area above the lid would be too confined. I need therefore to put the handle on a wider based teapot.

5 I chose this form because it meets the criteria of having a wide base for the handle, and a small narrow foot that lifts the form upwards. I make this form in two halves, joining when the clay is soft leatherhard.

6 A narrow thin spout enhances the elegant look.

7 A rough idea of the final piece. Note, even at this rough drawing stage, how the short fourth coil, acting as a thumb guide, lifts the perceived weight upwards.

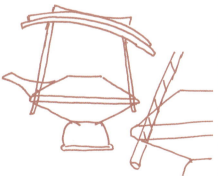

8 Rather than seating the handle's 'A' frame directly onto the teapot body, I like the idea of it extending a little below. I also hope that if the glazes move enough they will pool and create drips on the rod. I might try loading this area of the rod with glaze to encourage the effect.

9 I want the knob of the handle to reflect the bamboo handle structure; therefore I will construct it in a similar fashion using three small rolls of clay. Lifting the end will firstly give an uplifting impression to the lid, and secondly will create a flowing movement around the internal area of the handle and body.

10 When I join the two thrown halves of the body together, I create a small groove that will catch the flowing glazes on the top part of the body. Note, I could then play with cutting small gate holes in this groove to control where the glazes flood over the edge.

Secondly I put a groove in the base that I then wax, so that I have an area for the flowing glazes to run, rather than pouring onto the kiln shelf and ruining the pot.

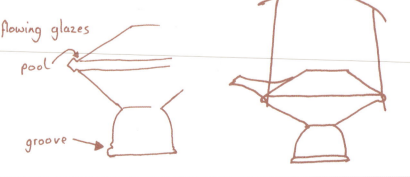

flowing glazes

pool

groove →

11 The height of the bamboo handle above the teapot body is crucial to the final appearance.

A Shows the teapot with a very low handle that looks squashed.

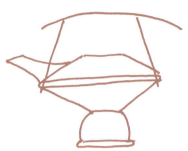

B Shows the teapot with a handle that effectively squares up the profile: this looks correct.

C Shows the teapot with a very tall handle, making it look lanky and weak.

11(b) is the way forward!

12 Again relating to the bamboo handle:

- If horizontal, it will create a sense of unity and harmony within the teapot.
- If the handle is higher toward the spout than the rear, it gives a sense of forward movement.
- If the handle is higher toward the rear, it does not seem right to me. I will not pursue this.

I have been making this style of teapot for several years now, and I realise how the variations in the positioning of the handle can have a dramatic effect on the final visual impression of the piece.

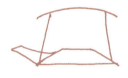

1

2

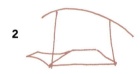

2)

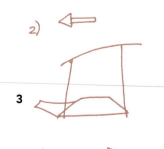

3

L₃

4 Contemporary Potters' Profiles

IN THIS CHAPTER we will examine the work of various potters, focusing on how they tackle the design, technical and aesthetic aspects of their teapots.

I mentioned earlier that there are so many excellent teapot-makers that the choice for this chapter was unlimited. However, in selecting the entries I tried to cover as many different making, decorating and firing techniques as possible, encompassing the wide spectrum of pots that are functional, non-functional and somewhere in-between. Many potters have included their clay and glaze recipes – these should be considered as good starting points for further development.

Chris Myers

(Australia)

Chris's teapots, like most of his work, are concerned with the play of light on the surface of the pot. His aim is to create an illusion of surface changes with different light intensities. In a room with natural light he would expect the form, colour and pattern to change as the day progresses and the light changes. Interestingly, he has found that when he photographs the same pot in different lights and coloured backgrounds, the change is so dramatic as to make it possible to

Stoneware teapot, height: 18 cm (7 in.). Thrown teapot with black glaze and slipcast handle, the pattern created with fine tape; sandblasted and glazed with multiple lustres.

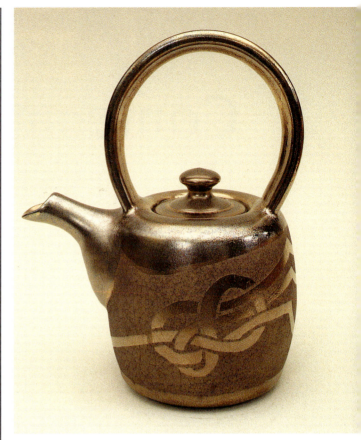

Stoneware teapot, height: 28 cm (11 in.). Thrown teapot with blue glaze, extruded handle and continuous knot pattern; sandblasted with gold and opal lustre.

Stoneware teapot, height: 26 cm (10.5 in.). Thrown teapot, with semi-matt celadon and extruded handle; pattern created from locked double sheet bend knot; sandblasted with gold and opal lustre.

believe that they are different pots! This is what Chris is trying to achieve. To accomplish this, Chris keeps the form fairly simple and cuts into the surface of the glaze using a sandblasting technique. The inspiration for his patterns is derived from anything that he sees around him, whether manmade or natural. The effect is completed by layering lustres over the whole surface and sandblasting specific areas so that there is a strong contrast between the matt areas and the glossy lustred areas. Chris sums it all by saying that he thinks of it as 'painting patterns with refractive light'.

Chris uses fine white stoneware and porcelain clays to make his teapots. The main consideration is that the body is white and does not interfere with the colour of the glaze. He does not want a clay that produces iron spots or speckles, as it spoils the way he

decorates, whereas a white clay keeps his glazes bright.

His teapots are all thrown on the wheel and assembled as normal, and are biscuit fired before glazing. Instead of waxing the galleries and base, he uses an aluminium based silver paint from the hardware store. This resists the glaze during glazing but also, when fired, produces a fine layer of alumina which stops the fine porcelain clay lids from sticking. Chris glazes his pots with simple glossy glazes. A range of colours are used, but the criteria is that they should be glossy and one single colour.

During glazing, he completely covers the pot with a plastic lagging tape and then draws his patterns onto the surface with a ballpoint pen. They are then cut out with a sharp blade, leaving parts of the pot still covered with the tape. Alternatively, he may use just

Stoneware teapot, height: 14 cm (5.5 in.). Thrown teapot with black glaze, extruded handle and geometric pattern, with the glaze completely removed in places; sandblasted, with multiple lustres.

Glaze Recipes

Black glaze, cone 10 (1300°C/2732°F), reduction

Potash feldspar	41.31
Kaolin	6.67
Ball clay	8.26
Whiting	13.42
Barium carbonate	2.00
Silica	18.50
Manganese dioxide	2.00
Cobalt oxide	1.00
Chromium oxide	0.50
Iron oxide	4.10

White glaze, cone 10 (1300°C/2732°F), oxidation

Potash feldspar	55.7
Kaolin	8.3
Whiting	13.3
Talc	12.7
Tin oxide	10.0

Deep blue glaze, cone 10 (1300°C/2732°F), reduction

Potash feldspar	25
Whiting	20
Kaolin	20
Silica	35
Cobalt oxide	1
Copper oxide	2

Green glaze, cone 10 (1300°C/2732°F), oxidation

Soda feldspar	40.0
Silica	27.0
Dolomite	16.7
Barium carbonate	8.0
Kaolin	4.0
Lithium carbonate	2.0
Tin oxide	2.0
Zinc oxide	0.3

These glazes are ball-milled to make sure that the colouring oxides do not speckle the glaze, but produce an even colour.

very fine masking tape to create the designs. Chris then uses a sandblaster to remove the surface of the exposed glaze, the rest being protected by the tape. This is why he prefers a glossy glaze, as the sandblaster produces a hard edge, contrasting the glossy glaze with the matt areas. Sometimes Chris removes the unmasked glaze completely down to the clay with the sandblaster, creating even more of a contrast. By combining both methods he can get a three-dimensional effect.

The remaining tape is then removed to expose the completed design, and the pot is washed with methylated spirits to take off any glue or dust.

Chris then uses a variety of lustres and fires them on to the pot to about 730°C (1346°F). Using several layers of lustres, he can achieve the colours he wants, a key factor being, of course, the colour of the initial glaze. Some of the pots may be lustred quite a few times before Chris is satisfied with the colours.

Claire Locker (Australia)

Claire lives and works in the hills near Mudgee in NSW, Australia, known for its rich clay and mineral deposits and its award-winning wines. She makes a range of thrown forms, mainly teapots, bowls and platters, in a range of sizes. Her forms are simple – conical-shaped teapots, bowls and platters with broad rims, which lend themselves to decoration.

Claire's great love is the combination of a thrown body covered with soft thin slabs, that are usually decorated with colour and texture prior to being assembled.

The choice of clay is crucial for this process; it needs to be a strong body and one that has hard dry strength as well as plasticity. The clay body Claire uses needs a coat of white slip prior to decoration, to brighten the colour. Her teapots evoke the image of dancing ladies, and the female in general. The first stage in the making process is to throw the inner form, which looks a little like a 'tailor's dummy' in dressmaking terms. Particular attention is paid to the finished shape where gentle curves lighten the appearance and accentuate the female form. The slabs that will make up the outer dress tend to make the form top heavy and therefore a

OPPOSITE PAGE Dancing Ladies, *handbuilt teapots, height: 35 cm (14 in.).*

TOP *Claire Locker adjusting the skirt on her teapot.*
ABOVE *Handbuilt teapot, height: 35 cm (14 in.).*

stable foot is required. Claire says that the main points to be considered are balance, proportion and height. The lid is thrown and a slab knob is added. As the lid sits deep in the gallery, the knob is emphasised. The spout is rolled around a suitable form (sometimes a piece of dowel and at other times a tapered paintbrush), depending on the outcome required. The handle is made from a rolled and decorated slab.

Claire rolls out at least four slabs of clay 30 x 30 x 0.2 cm (12 x 12 x 0.1 in.), which are then decorated with at least three coloured slips or underglazes, varying in tone between light and dark. These need to be thick and of even consistency (uneven application leads to uneven drying, resulting in cracking). When the shine disappears from the slab, she places a cloth over the painted slab and rolls it with moderate strength; this impresses the fabric texture into it and softens the design. The cloth is actually rubber-backed curtain material that gives the appearance of fabric. Handling this thin slab can cause problems, so to keep the freshness Claire uses cloths to handle the clay.

In a similar fashion to dressmaking, Claire cuts the desired shapes of the dress, starting from the waist up. On each piece she smooths the edges of the cut clay with the cloth pleat to the desired length and adds it to the teapot (tailor's dummy) form. She repeats the process to create the skirt. Lastly, she adds strips of clay around the waist as a belt, which neatens as well as decorates. Claire pays particular attention to the edges of the skirts, as these are critical to the overall professional finish of the piece. The viewer immediately sees any rough edges.

The final teapot comprises many pieces of clay, with each piece varying in its own water content. This is a critical point, which can cause uneven drying, with cracking and pieces falling off. To prevent this, Claire covers the teapot with plastic for at least two weeks. This seems a long time, but it solves the problem.

Depending on the desired finish, she sometimes glazes the total piece, at other times only the undecorated areas, using a clear shiny glaze. The firing temperature varies from 1120°C–1280°C (2048°F–2336°) depending on the clay used.

David Frith
(Wales)

David works with his wife Margaret in their workshop (Brookhouse Pottery) in Denbighshire, Wales. His perception of form and function has developed over the years with the consequential evolution of the nature of the piece. David still considers himself to be a repetition potter because the pots spring from familiarity of form, and the integral nature of the materials used, although he now works on more individual pieces.

The materials are selected and prepared in his workshop. The clay is based on Devonshire ball clays, china clay, feldspar with silica sand or grog. It is a light firing clay, hard and durable and a rich base for celadon glazes. The return to wood firing has given an added dimension to the pieces with the fly ash on the unglazed surfaces giving a rich toasting and it contrasts well with the unglazed surface.

Teapot-making is so critical because it demands a total balance and unity. There are so many considerations involved with the scaling of the lid, spout and handle to the thrown body. There is a certain comfort and elegance in pouring tea from a handsome pot. It is wholesome, ritualistic, and calms the spirit. If the pot is good it brings delight to the day.

Making sequence

1 *Paddling the cylinder prior to throwing out.*
2 *Collaring in the neck to form the lid seating.*
3 *Forming the lid seating.*
4 *Using a throwing stick to form the belly of the teapot.*
5 *Trimming the surplus clay from the bottom of the teapot.*
6 *Using the fingers to finish the foot-ring.*
7 *Drilling the sieve holes.*
8 *Pulling the side handle.*
9 *Bending the handle back on itself to give added strength and also make it comfortable to hold.*
10 *Smoothing the handle into the teapot body.*
11 *Finished unfired teapot with spout and a pulled side handle.*

FAR RIGHT *Paddled teapot with side handle, height: 15 cm (6 in.). Celadon and ash glazed.*

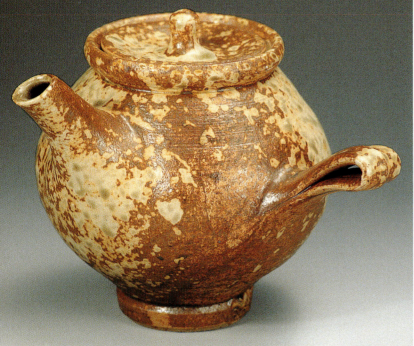

TOP LEFT *Teapot, height: 18 cm (7 in.), decorated with tenmoku and ash glaze.*

ABOVE *Side-handled teapot, height: 15 cm (6 in.), ash glazed.*

TOP RIGHT *Teapot, height: 21.5 cm (8½ in.), decorated with tenmoku and ash glaze.*

RIGHT *Faceted teapot, height: 23 cm (9 in.). This teapot was faceted when leatherhard. Decorated with celadon and Kaki glaze.*

Derek Emms
(England)

Derek lives and works in Stone, Stoke-on-Trent, England. He makes a wide range of domestic stoneware but is widely known for his teapots. Derek is often regarded as 'the teapot-maker' in England and Chapter Two, which covers the making of the standard teapot, shows Derek at work. He has been making teapots for over 50 years and his experience will improve invaluable to students of ceramics.

Many potters nowadays use the teapot form as a basis for artistic expression, some push the boundaries beyond what is regarded as a teapot! Derek, however, has focused on and fully mastered the classic domestic teapot.

ABOVE *Stoneware teapot, height: 12.5 cm (5 in.). The teapot body has been incised using a metal tool, creating a rhythmic pattern. Initially Derek dissects the pot into 12 equal parts, and then carves the pattern in each segment. The celadon glaze pools in the grooves enhance the decoration.*
BELOW *Porcelain teapots (1-cup, 1-pint and 4-pint teapot).*

TOP *Stoneware teapot, height: 12.5 cm (5 in.). The teapot body has been thrown slightly thicker than required and, when leatherhard, has been faceted using a cheese cutter. The teapot is glazed with a tenmoku glaze which characteristically breaks at the edges, enhancing the form. Derek encourages this breaking by very carefully rubbing his finger over the edges, removing a minute portion of glaze.*

ABOVE *Stoneware teapot, height: 12.5 cm (5 in.). Tenmoku glaze and a rutile pattern brushed on.*

RIGHT *Stoneware teapot, height: 12.5 cm (5 in.). Incised vertically with a metal tool and glazed with a tenmoku glaze.*

Glaze Recipe

Tenmoku glaze

FFF Feldspar	62
Whiting	10
Flint	19
Ball clay	9
Red iron oxide	8

Celadon glaze

Feldspar	40
Flint	30
Whiting	20
China clay	10
Talc	5
Red iron oxide	1
Zinc oxide	5
Molochite (200s mesh)	5

Walter Keeler (England)

Walter has been making individual teapots for over 20 years, playing and pushing the parameters of the form, creating new and exciting ideas for the rest of us to follow. In the last 7 years he has shifted his focus and developed a stunning earthenware range, being inspired by Staffordshire Creamware of the 18th century. However, Walter continues to make his unique style of salt-glazed teapots. An underlying feature is that they are tight and precise forms, which, when salt glazed, create the beautifully textured surfaces that complement the form so well.

Most of Walter's teapots start off in his sketchbook (*see p.67*), where, as you can see, various aspects of the idea are explored. His teapots often incorporate simple forms in complex relationships; for example, the handle is constructed from two coils of different widths, joined near the base. Solid handles would be too heavy so to compensate for this Walter makes them hollow. At this point any technical aspect can be prepared for, i.e. has he the correct dies to extrude a handle for this style of teapot?

Earthenware teapot, height: 22.5 cm (9 in.).

Making sequence

1 When leatherhard, the body is carefully attached to a batt with a soft coil of clay. This batt has been mounted on the wheel with wads of clay under one edge, presenting the teapot at an angle.

2 A sharp tool is used to cut an eccentric opening for the lid, and final adjustment is made to the diameter with a bent section of Surform blade. A coil is then added to the edge, and the outside defined with a square-edged metal rib.

3 To make the spout, a thin slab of clay is folded and bent to roughly the shape of the plaster mould. This is positioned in the mould and gently pressed in. Note that the mould is made longer that the required length of the spout, allowing the tapering spout to be cut at various points, giving a range of individual spouts.

4 Using a small wet brush to coax the slab into the mould.

5 Cutting along the edge with a sharp knife.

6 Preparing the mirror mould in the same manner, applying slip to the edges and offering the two moulds together.

Photograph sequence by John Wheeldon.

7 Pressing the mould together firmly.

8 Initially sealing the joint from the inside using a finger. Using a bent stick the joints can be sealed further up the mould, a process requiring considerable time and patience.

9 Firming up the clay in the mould using a hot-air gun.

10 Carefully removing the spout. The joint down the centre line of the spout is cleaned up. Sometimes fettled right back to the spout, at other times a feature is made of this thin line which is beautifully picked up in the rich salt glazing.

11 The handle is made from two round-section hollow extrusions. These are bent and left to firm up. Joining these together by butting the edges together does not create a tight strong join and causes problems down the line. To overcome this, Walter drills a precise counterhole into the end of the thicker coil. Slurry is added and the thinner coil fits precisely into this hole. The join it creates is both strong mechanically and tight aesthetically.

12 The angle of spring of the handle from the teapot body is very important to the final form. Presenting the handle in this way allows Walter to resolve this issue.

13 Sketching the cross-section of the teapot onto a sheet of paper allows Walter to line up the teapot handle precisely before cutting with a wire and bow. Notice how he uses a set square to ensure the cut is perfectly vertical.

14 When complete, the teapot is wrapped in polythene and left for a few days to slowly dry out. After biscuiting, the pots are selectively dipped into a biscuit slip or engobe (60 feldspar; 40 china clay). When the clay body is exposed, a strong 'orange-peel' texture develops due to the sand contained in the clay mix. The engobe masks this with a layer of finer particles that are lower in silica, resulting in a smooth texture from the salting. Colour is achieved by spraying pigment over the whole piece (both dipped and undipped areas). The pigment might be a black stain or a mixture of oxides.

TOP *Salt-glazed teapot.*
ABOVE *Salt-glazed teapot, height: 22.5 cm (9 in.).*
RIGHT *Salt-glazed teapot height: 22.5 cm (9 in.).*

TOP *Earthenware*
teapot, height: 22.5 cm (9 in.).
BOTTOM LEFT *Earthenware*
teapot, height: 22.5 cm (9 in.).
RIGHT *Salt-glazed teapot,*
height: 25 cm (10 in.).
Photograph by James Robson.

Joanna Howells (Wales)

Joanna has been attracted to the qualities of porcelain ever since college – its whiteness, translucency, extreme smoothness, and its clear colour response to glazes. These qualities have traditionally been exploited in a rather crisp and static way. Joanna prefers to

RIGHT *Porcelain teapot, height: 25 cm (10 in.), with metal handle.*
BELOW *Porcelain teapots, height: 25 cm (10 in.). Note how the metal handles mirror the teapot body shape.*

ABOVE *Porcelain teapots.*

Making sequence

1 *Joanna has thrown the standard teapot body with an extra flange at the shoulder for the metal handle retainers. Using a thin wire she carefully cuts away the surplus clay flange.*

2 *Applying the slip using a kidney, building up a flowing pattern around the body.*

3 *Cutting into the slip with a modified (serrated edge) rubber kidney. Again Joanna is continuing with this theme of movement. Subsequently, the teapot is assembled as normal, glazed in a blue celadon and fired in a gas kiln to cone 10 (1300°C/2372°F).*

4 *The forged stainless-steel handle* from the blacksmith is heated using an oxy-acetylene torch to soften the metal in the centre of the handle – only about 2.5 cm (1 in.) of metal is heated in this way.

5 *Holding the cooler ends in (even though the centre of the metal* handle is extremely hot the ends are cool) Joanna bends and positions the handle in the retainers at the shoulder. Warning: care must be taken here, as the central part of the handle is very hot.

6 *Lastly, the handle is quenched in cold water.*

work in a dynamic but simple and direct manner, working into the surface of a freshly thrown piece by texturing with slip and impressed marks. This treatment results in a visual and tactile softness that belies the hardness of the material.

Pinning down sources of inspiration is an approximate enterprise, especially as she tries to avoid post-hoc justifications. She admires ancient Cycladic sculpture and early Chinese porcelain. The strongest visual influence at present is the interaction of wind, water and coastline near her South Wales home. The use of metal for handles resulted from mixed media experiments in the late 1990s. Using forged iron was a radical choice, bringing together materials with conflicting cultural connotations – iron associated with manufacturing or rusticity, porcelain with refined society or imperial splendour. Yet they share much at the level of process and product – both passing through fire and possessing underlying qualities of strength and hardness.

John Calver (England)

John lives and works on the Lancashire–Cumbria border, England. He makes a variety of domestic stoneware pieces, all decorated in his usual style.

His teapot starts as a thrown cylinder without a top, the form is then altered dramatically into a triangular shape by pushing a bamboo profile tool against the base while it spins on the wheel.

This process creates a sensuous bulge. The top is thrown separately and added when firm, the rim being smoothed and modelled using a thumbnail and wash-leather. The lid and spout are then thrown in the standard way. The spout is added at this stage.

John adds feet to many of his teapots. Unlike many potters he adds four feet rather than three,

Stoneware teapot, height: 25 cm (10 in.).

Teapot by John Calver.

however, the back two feet are very close and effectively act as one. The feet are made from coils rolled on a textured surface, squashed and beaten into shape. The end result is a curved foot with claws. The overall impression has an animalistic quality and works very well.

The loopover handle completes the piece. The stripes on the handle emphasise the form and balance the textured feet. The handle is made from a twisted wire loop that is wiggled through a slab of clay and then stiffened over a curved surface. When firm, the handle is offered up to the teapot and held at the right height so that it looks correct; it is then cut and added to the teapot. The size of the loop handle is crucial to the final overall appearance of the piece, and John takes special care to get this right. The handle leans slightly forward to give a sense of movement and life, mirroring the forward movement of the pouring tea.

When the teapot is leatherhard, John slip trails (using an iron-bearing slip) and sponges on a floral repeat pattern (using an iron/rutile slip). During the firing the iron will bleed into, and sometimes through, some of the glazes on top, to give a matt metallic finish. This process is dependent on many factors and

John making his wire-cut handles.

clean the surfaces of any glaze.

The final stage is the firing in an oil-fired kiln. The temperature and level of reduction can be controlled by the flame path through it. John describes the kiln as another creative tool and exploits its characteristics to the full. During the firing some of his glazes have a tendency to flow, especially down the vertical grooves on the feet; for this reason all his work is fired on wads. The kiln is fired to miniature cone 11 (1320°C/ 2408°F) including a long 10-hour reduction cycle. The last 30 minutes is in oxidation to brighten the colours. For John, the driving force is the uniqueness of each piece.

Glaze Recipes

Using an iron-bearing, lightly grogged stoneware body which fires grey.

Semi-matt glaze

Talc	11.2
Whiting	20.5
Feldspar	32.2
China clay	16.6
Flint	19.5
Rutile	8.3
Calcium chloride	1.0
Cobalt oxide	0.75

Dry matt blue glaze

Feldspar	50
Barium carbonate	45
Ball clay	5
Tin oxide	1
Rutile	4
Cobalt carbonate	1

results in a certain randomness. Where there is uncertainty there is a potential to reach beyond expectation, but also to disappoint – 'life is like that!'

At the glazing stage, John is aiming for a glaze finish that looks rich and thick, but not so thick as to prevent bleeding through of the iron decoration beneath. Creating variety in the thickness of the glazes gives John a further subtlety of decoration in his piece.

The pieces are waxed on the rim and feet. The inside is glazed and left to dry. John is a keen rock-climber so adopting a classical grip

he places his fist in the teapot gallery, and tightening the fist, grips the pot very securely. Holding the pot upside down he pours the first glaze over the pot, and by rotating the wrist he continues to pour, thereby creating a variety of thicknesses. The pot is held for 30 seconds or so until the surface loses its watery sheen. A second glaze is then poured over. Using this technique a variety of thickness can be achieved, giving a range of texture.

The lid is fired with the teapot. John does not use alumina to separate the pieces and prevent the lid sticking, but does meticulously

Margaret Frith (Wales)

Margaret works with her husband David in their Brookhouse Pottery workshop in Wales. Margaret regards teapot-making as a very complex sequence of skilled processes, each a unique part, which must be united to make the whole. The potter must balance the separate pieces and create an entity.

Margaret makes her teapots to be used, and never makes one that does not work. It is important to her that the pot pours. She says that the craft of making is in her blood and a teapot that does not function annoys her! Margaret works with a porcelain body, which she makes herself. It is very plastic and throws well but has a high shrinkage and can distort. It shows no mercy – so if the form is not good, the flaws will be exaggerated.

The teapots are fired by gas or wood to stoneware temperature 1280°C (2336°F) using celadon and iron glazes. Sometimes Margaret combines these glazed areas with ashed unglazed areas. She often uses a fireclay wash to give the body more depth especially over the impressed areas. The glazes each have their own temperature range and the firing is critical. The glazes must be applied just at the right thickness, leaving a little time

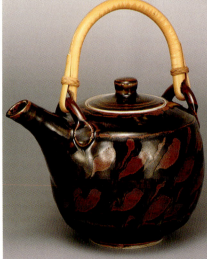

in-between applications of additional glazes. Wax decoration is often used between the layers and this is sometimes combined with glaze trailing.

ABOVE *Porcelain teapot with cane handle, height: 21 cm (8¼ in.). Thrown and paddled with an impression of a leaf motif. After biscuiting, the piece is dipped in a fireclay wash, and a green celadon and dark blue overglaze are poured over. Note the tight little spout.*
LEFT *Porcelain teapot with cane handle, height: 21 cm (8¼ in.). Glazed in a tessha glaze (a variation of a tenmoku) with a wax decoration then applied. The pot is then dipped in thin green celadon overglaze. During the firing, the green celadon reacts with the tessha to give a bright tenmoku, leaving the tessha brushwork.*

RIGHT *Porcelain teapot, height: 12.5 cm (5 in.). Thrown and paddled with an impression of a leaf motif. After biscuiting, the piece is dipped in a fireclay wash, and then glazed with a deep blue celadon glaze. An ash/clay mixture is then sponged on which, after firing, gives a salt-glazed effect.*

ABOVE *Porcelain teapot, height: 12.5 cm (5 in.). After biscuiting, the piece is dipped in a fireclay wash, and a pale blue celadon is then poured over, creating decorative areas of the raw fireclay. Japanese brushwork is applied to this area using a cobalt mix.*

RIGHT *Porcelain teapot, height: 12.5 cm (5 in.) After biscuiting, the piece is dipped in a fireclay wash, and then a blue glaze is sponged on. Further decoration includes bold iron brushwork and copper-red trailed dots.*

Morgen Hall (Wales)

Morgen's teapots are thrown and turned from high-firing red earthenware decorated with cobalt-blue slip and tin glazed. Although the teapots are thrown (including the spouts), the emphasis is on the turning to achieve near burnished surfaces on any unglazed areas. The fine detail, including beaded rouletted pattern, is applied using brass book-binding tools. After turning the body and lid, the spout and handles are applied. The handles are initially extruded and then pulled to a taper. Whilst the teapot is still leatherhard, stencils are applied to the surface of the clay and latex resist is painted on any surface that does not require slip, such as the foot-ring, handle and gallery. Cobalt-blue slip is then sponged over the surface. In

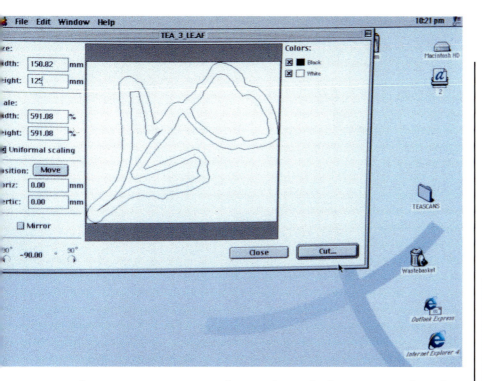

ABOVE *Computer monitor screen showing the tea leaf pattern as outline about to be cut into a stencil on a plotter-cutter.*

OPPPOSITE PAGE
INSET *Earthenware teapot, height: 18 cm (7 in.), by Morgen Hall, Cardiff, Wales. Photo by Patricia Aithie.*
BELOW *Thrown and turned leatherhard teapot, with plotter-cut stencils and latex on foot-ring, spout, handle and gallery.*

a few minutes the slip is dry enough to remove the stencils. Slip-trailed pattern work is applied at this stage on some pots.

Morgen's stencils are derived from actual tea leaves. Soaked tea leaves are placed directly on the glass of a scanner, scanned into a computer and made into black and white images. The outlines are then selected, sizes chosen and the leaf shapes then cut on a computer-linked plotter-cutter (the same machine used by most signwriters today).

This process allows the actual line of leaf tea to be used as pattern. The CAD-CAM process allows any scale of stencil to be made from 2 mm to 200 m (0.1 in. to 666 ft) or more. Stencils can be made from a variety of material up to 1 mm (0.1 in.) thick. Morgen initially began plotter-cutting stencils from newspaper because she had previously used them to make scissor-cut stencils. The newspaper unfortunately blunts the expensive blades for the plotter-cutters so she now cuts stencils from the same sticky backed vinyl that signwriters use.

The pots are biscuit fired to 1000°C (1832°F) then dipped in tin glaze. A rutile-based glaze stain is lightly sponged onto the powdery glaze surface prior to glaze firing to 1120°C (2048°F) in an electric kiln.

The teapots are intended to be a pleasure to use with spouts that pour well and handles that are comfortable to hold. Morgen's influences include British tea wares from the 1750s, thrown with rouletted detail.

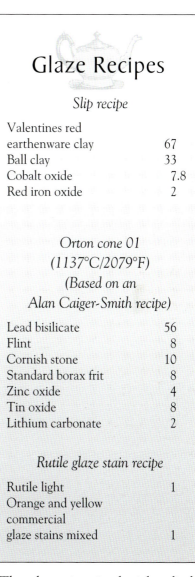

Glaze Recipes

Slip recipe

Valentines red earthenware clay	67
Ball clay	33
Cobalt oxide	7.8
Red iron oxide	2

*Orton cone 01
(1137°C/2079°F)
(Based on an
Alan Caiger-Smith recipe)*

Lead bisilicate	56
Flint	8
Cornish stone	10
Standard borax frit	8
Zinc oxide	4
Tin oxide	8
Lithium carbonate	2

Rutile glaze stain recipe

Rutile light	1
Orange and yellow commercial glaze stains mixed	1

The above is mixed with a little tin glaze and a lot of water. The stain must be applied *very* thinly on the glaze surface.

Mick Casson (England)

Mick reviewed his profile shortly before he sadly passed away. He worked with his wife Sheila in Upton Bishop in the foothills of Wales and made teapots for over 30 years. In the 1960s he used to make them in batches of 30. The teapots were tenmoku-glazed stoneware, classically spherical with cane handles. These teapots were not only designed to be functional but also to be made quickly and efficiently. So on the first day he would throw the 30 bodies and 30 lids. Then, on the second day, he would assemble the constituent parts and finish them. The spouts were then thrown at this point and joined straight onto the body wet. This method was new to the pottery world, but saved so much time and effort cutting, carving and shaving the leatherhard spout.

More recently, Mick made teapots like the one shown below in batches of about six, using either stoneware or porcelain clay. As stoneware is a more accommodating clay, the porcelain teapots need a few extra stages in the making process. The body was thrown in the usual way, compressing the clay on the base. The gallery was thrown and the edge again compressed to make it slightly thicker than the rest of

Salt-glazed teapot, height: 20 cm (8 in.).

the body, making it strong both visually and physically. To emphasise the gallery and lid there is a sharp change in direction. Where the curve of the body changes upwards to form the gallery, a line was inscribed into the clay that accentuates this. At the base of the body, Mick would chamfer the edge, and then score round the base. Scoring these lines at the top and bottom of the body is clearly stating, 'Here are the edges of the pot'. Mick himself used to say, 'emphasise the beginning and the end, and the rest will take care of itself.' The body was left uncut on the batt, and Mick wired off the pot on the second day. The lid was thrown upside down in the usual manner.

On the following day, both the body and lid were at the soft leatherhard stage. If the clay was porcelain, then the first job was to recheck with callipers that the lid and gallery still fit. Porcelain has an irritating tendency to move a little. If a correction was necessary then Mick would adjust by either wetting the gallery and re-throwing, or turning a little off the lid.

The batt with the unwired body was placed on the wheel and became the natural chuck on which to turn the lid. The edges may need to be wetted slightly to aid adhesion, but this is usually not required as the clay is soft leatherhard. Mick's lids always have a lug on them to prevent the lid from falling off when the tea is poured; this lug was put directly opposite the hole in the lid so that the user knows where it is.

The majority of Mick's latest teapots have two handles. This is a personal preference, conjuring up a more ceremonial aspect to pouring the tea, by using both hands to hold the teapot. When holding the pot, you tend to use just your fingertips and not grasp the handle in the palm of your hand. The end result is that the side handle can be made quite small, giving the teapot a more compact and rounded form. Mick fired with salt and as a result any marks on the clay tend to be highlighted in the firing process. He emphasised the joining of the handles by sweeping strokes of his thumbnail, which picks up the salt decoratively.

The spout was thrown on the wheel. For aesthetic

Porcelain teapot, height: 20 cm (8 in.).

reasons Mick liked the end of the spout to fan outwards slightly. This can cause considerable problems with the pouring, resulting in the liquid splurging out of the spout rather than emerging in a focused stream. This is overcome slightly by compressing the flared-out spout into an oval. (Technically your oval should have the same area as the circle and will thereby cause no backpressure.)

Having thrown the spout, it was assembled straight onto the body, and at this point bent downwards into a lovely curve.

The spout was left for a while to firm up before being cut in a cockerel fashion, which he described as his homage to Michael Cardew's teapots of the early 1920s.

After the spout and handle had been added, the pot was wired off the batt with a very thin piece of steel wire so that it cut cleanly and left as little

LEFT *Porcelain teapot, height: 20 cm (8 in.).*

OPPOSITE PAGE

1 *The bottom of the handle is attached to the body.*
2 *A small piece of clay is melded into the joint to strengthen it and also to create an aesthetically more pleasing join. Mick finishes off his handles with his characteristic sweeping marks to give the teapot a sense of movement.*
3 *Smoothing and tidying up around the handle.*
4 *Carefully marking the top/bottom of the cockerel spout.*
5 *Having marked the top and bottom, the side edges are marked. The spout is then cut. Notice how the hands support each other.*
6 *Cutting away a second chunk to finish the cockerel spout.*

clay on the batt as possible.

The teapot was turned upside down and the galley is placed onto a small 7.5 cm (3 in.) porcelain bowl. Supporting it in this way allowed Mick to add the feet without knocking the handle and spout. At this point the feet would be added. Mick put three feet on these teapots – two feet to the front of the pot and one behind, for two reasons:

• This teapot has a small side handle and therefore the spout seems to draw the weight forward. To accommodate this, Mick put two feet towards the front of the teapot and one at the rear

• The one at the rear is directly below the handle and helps to carry on its visual movement

At this juncture Mick had to decide to either tap the base of the pot upwards, as in normal workshop practice, or because this pot has feet, tap the base downwards from inside in order to emphasise the shape.

Mick used to raw glaze his pots, but lately preferred to biscuit them. After biscuiting, the inside of the teapot was glazed with a manganese glaze. This is a thick slop glaze and therefore required Mick to blow down the spout in order to ensure that the sieve holes were not blocked. When

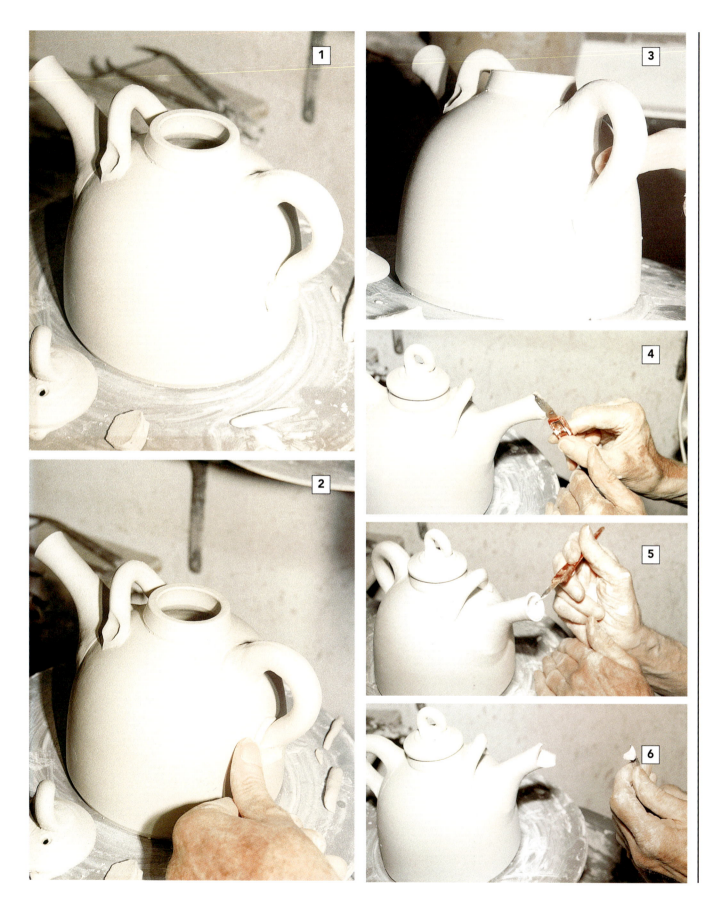

the glaze was dry, the outside of the pot was then dipped in slip (HVAR 50: china clay 50). The lid was fired in place, with alumina rather than wadding. The teapot was then salt fired in a wood or gas kiln to above 1300°C (2372°F), cone 12 down.

After the firing, Mick used a large cold chisel and hammer and very gently tapped the lid/gallery. Amazingly, the lid separated cleanly. If the lid was a little tight in the gallery, Mick used a carborundum grinding paste (ball clay and 120s mesh carborundum powder) and gently turned the lid around until he had a beautifully smooth finish.

Peter Ilsley (England)

Peter lives and works in Northamptonshire, England, during the summer. In the winter he lives in southern Spain where he throws and biscuit fires his porcelain pieces in the sunshine, ready to bring back in the spring and gloss fire. In the past he has made a wide range of stoneware, porcelain, raku and crystalline work but nowadays the majority of his time is focused on macro-crystalline glazes. This type of work is mainly to be found on his bottles, vases and bowls, although he occasionally decorates his teapots in this way too.

This is a very specialist decorative technique and it is interesting to see how Peter applies it to a teapot form. There are several additional parameters that Peter has to consider in designing his teapot to take the crystalline glaze due to its fluidity.

Firstly, the teapots are thrown on the wheel. Peter keeps the form smooth and clean to facilitate glaze flow and crystal growth. The teapot's catcher (a dish thrown to catch surplus glaze) must also be thrown at the same time as the teapot body so that they contract together and can be turned to fit the base of the teapot precisely.

The pieces are fired to between 1280°C (2336°F) and 1300°C (2372°F), at which point the glaze is at its most fluid and is actually flowing slowly down the pot. To compensate for this Peter applies most of the glaze to the top third of the pot, which acts as a reservoir during the firing. This application of glaze can be up to 1.2 cm (½ in.) thick! At peak, the temperature is reduced quite quickly to approximately 1080°C–1100°C (1976°F–2012°F) where the soak commences, lasting between two and five hours. The crystals develop in the glassy matrix.

Peter has chosen a continuous foot for the base of the teapot because it is the best type of footring to accommodate the flow of glaze. Also, aesthetically it creates a beautiful flowing curve to the base of the pot. To prevent the glazes flowing and sticking the pot onto the kiln shelf, Peter sits the pot on a catcher, which collects the glaze run-off. The most important feature of the catcher is that it must be the same diameter as the foot-ring; it is therefore an important part of his teapot-making process. The firing causes the catcher to become welded to the pot with glaze and this has to be removed with the aid of a needle-flame blowlamp.

The lid is fired with the teapot to ensure that it fits. To prevent the crystalline glaze overflowing from the edge of the lid and onto the teapot body, Peter grooves the edge of the lid so that it has in effect its own catcher.

In order to achieve the full visual effect of the crystals it is advisable to have a pure white background, and for this purpose Peter uses Audrey Blackman porcelain (Valentine Clay Products Ltd.) which is very white, translucent and good for throwing.

The entire decorative effect is based on the growth of the crystals in the glaze, which Peter describes by saying 'crystal growth is in the lap of the gods; it is a trinity of form, glaze application and complex firing schedule'. He loves the completely random effect of the macro-crystalline glazes, though I think he can control it a little more than he admits! Initially, the inside is glazed with a hard, shiny, serviceable glaze, usually a tenmoku, which is a fairly thick slop that is applied slightly thinner than usual to prevent pooling. The glaze, decoration and shape of the pot must all work together in harmony to create the final piece.

Dripping spouts are described by Peter as 'a pain in the arse' and I think we would all agree with that! To avoid this, after the spout is thrown and attached when soft leatherhard in the standard way, he cuts the end at an angle and thins it out with a drill, creating a thinner edge to cut off the flow of tea whist maintaining a protected area around it. Peter believes the spout is a key element to the overall image of the teapot and must look well-balanced and appropriate.

Macro-crystalline teapot, height: 22.5 cm (9 in.).

His handles are pulled, extruded or rolled, depending on what is right for that particular teapot. The lid is turned and a knob applied that is compatible with the handle. The space created between handle and body is mirrored in the small strap handle on top of the lid. This strap handle creates a significant aesthetic impact on the piece. If you mask out this handle on the photo you will see what I mean. Peter makes it is very clear that the relationship of the spout,

handle and lid give the teapot character and reflect the personality of the maker.

When making standard ware, Peter once-fires, glazing the bone dry work. However, he biscuits his teapots because the teapot is a complex form, and the thick once-fire glazes could potentially open up the joins. His work is fired in oxidation to 1280°C–1300°C (2336°F–2372°F) with a 2 to 4 hour soak on the cooling cycle, to allow the crystals to grow at between 1100°C–1000°C (2012°F– 1832°F).

Peter Meanley (Ireland)

Peter has made only spouted pouring vessels for 18 years, all of which are salt glazed. He estimates that he may have produced between 500 and 600 during this time. All his teapots have an individual character but are normally based upon a theme. He used to call all the vessels he made 'teapots'. Now he calls them 'spouted pouring vessels'. This provides him with more latitude to abstract his forms and reassess the various parts and their relationship with each other. Nevertheless, they still have to be capable of containing and dispensing liquid.

Peter collects 18th-century English and German salt-glazed ware, Whieldon and Chinese redware. These teach him many of the processes and qualities he hopes to achieve in his own work. Detail is very important, as is the relationship between the various parts. Peter believes that we have forgotten much about the work of our predecessors – he once spent

Salt-glazed teapot, height: 17 cm (7 in.), pouring from the base. Wheel-thrown body and legs, press-moulded spout and extruded handle. Photograph by Errol Forbes.

several hours at the V&A museum in London working out the sequence and methodology of a Tang decorated vessel, and eventually established 14 stages in the application of the slips!

The main consideration for Peter is that all his teapots should function well. The idea for the form comes first; he plays a lot on paper to hone the essence of his idea. At this point he is already considering the spout and water flow. Although Peter

is adamant that his teapots have to be capable of being used, he does make concessions with the lid, and may include only a small lid opening for purely aesthetic reasons.

Peter uses 1145 white stoneware (Potclays), as it throws well and is still strong when cone 10 (1305°C/2381°F) is flat. Most of Peter's teapot bodies are thrown. However, he quite often offsets some of the thrown parts or even inverts the body or places a false profile base. These various techniques give Peter a wide spectrum of forms from which to work.

LEFT Cadogan Pouring Vessel, *height: 18 cm (7 in.).* *Wheel-thrown body, comprising strainer, press-moulded spout and handle. This teapot is filled from the base and derived from a 17th-century wine ewer.* Photograph by Errol Forbes.
BELOW Plasticine Pouring Vessel, *height: 13 cm (5 in.).* *Wheel-thrown body, press-moulded spout and handle with coloured clay sprigs.* Photograph by Errol Forbes.

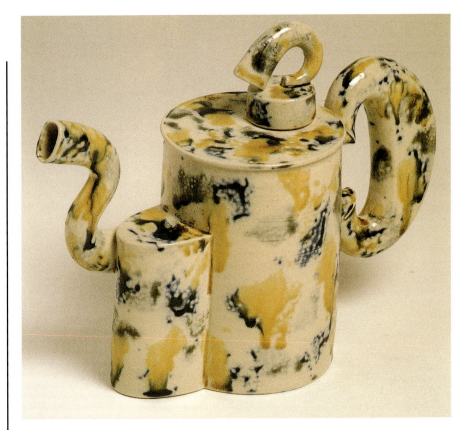

Spouts, handles and finials are often made from two-part press moulds, with the original modelled in plasticine. Peter loves the process of cutting up and reassembling parts; for example, a handle may be constructed from several individual parts. He slabs very little, although occasionally he uses a sheet of clay for larger spout forms. Smaller spouts and handles are made solid and then cut away with a wire-ended tool. Many of Peter's teapots have feet, though he often incorporates the handle or spout to also act as the third foot.

Peter describes his teapots as having personalities – they are like people, some want to turn away, others are poised ready to act. The teapot body is the key facilitator; it provides a base on which the personalities can be exhibited.

The handle and spout are focal points that complement one another. A large, active spout with a tiny handle provides a sharp contrast in scale and can create a shock, resulting in a new aesthetic look to the piece. Alternatively, a dominant handle needs to be balanced with a smaller spout. Peter refers to 'active spouts' requiring 'passive handles' or vice versa.

According to Peter, the teapot body often requires a secondary interest of a randomly placed small sprig to balance it up.

His teapots are decorated with slips, which are always applied on biscuit (1000°C/1832°F) and after copious testing he knows how much the salt is likely to affect them. The slips are very simple, ranging from a 50:50 grolleg china clay/Hyplas 71 ball clay, through to 100% Hyplas 71. The high silica Hyplas readily takes the salt and encourages the glaze to run more easily. Oxides of iron, manganese, cobalt and chrome are used to modify the above. Blue might be cobalt 1.5% and red iron oxide 4%; turquoise might be cobalt 1.5% and chromium 3%; the addition of a further 10% of manganese will alter the blues to dark browns, black, lilacs.

Some of Peter's vessels are what he describes as 'tight' and need to be sprayed with a slip. Others require a looser application, creating an 'opening up' of the orange peel in the kiln. On these vessels he may squirt or pour the slips. The *Celery Leaf Pouring Vessel* is decorated with coloured slips that have been applied using a celery leaf.

Finally, the pots are salt glazed, Peter salts at cone 3 (1170°C/2138°F) through to cone 10 (1305°C/2381°F) then he 'hangs in' and flattens cone 10. For the final 10 minutes he opens up the damper to oxidise and ensure a good quality gloss surface. After switching off the kiln, he rapidly cools it down to 950°C (1742°F),

then closes it up. During the firing, Peter uses very light reduction to full oxidation, as he wants the whiteness of the body to enhance the colours of the slips.

Placement of the teapot is very important in the kiln. The side of the teapot facing the firebox will take more flame and the glazes here will therefore be a little more fluid. In addition, the spout tends to pull towards the flame. Peter can use this effect to straighten a spout that has pulled a little off true during biscuit firing.

ABOVE *Salt-glazed teapot, height: 17 cm (6½ in.). Wheel-thrown body and parts. The 'lid' on the body is false, as the liquid enters the teapot via the handle. The sieve for this teapot is also mounted in the handle.* Photograph by Errol Forbes.
LEFT *Peter examining the profile and aesthetic balance of the leatherhard teapot.*

Petra Reynolds (England)

Petra slab-builds a variety of domestic teapots, the construction commencing with a series of paper templates (similar to dressmaking). She cuts around these templates and, once the clay slabs are the correct consistency, mitres the edges, and folds or bends them, then joins the slabs to form the desired shape. It is important to create a strong edge and joint; Petra achieves this by compressing the clay with her fingers and then a small roller. Rims are shaped and softened with a sponge and sometimes beaten thicker with a wooden edge. Petra makes the handles from slabs rolled into tubes (hollow inside). A small pinhole is used to stop the handle blowing off during firing.

Once leatherhard, Petra decorates the teapot using a variety slips and glazes. Initially she layers colour using brushwork or pouring, occasionally adding contrast with paper resist. These marks and patterns provide the canvas for a more linear decoration which is achieved by a form of print making. Slip (usually black) is brushed onto sheets of newspaper and left to go tacky. The slipped newspaper pieces are then placed onto the pots. Petra transfers the slip from the paper to the pot by rubbing the paper with her fingers. She raw glazes the insides of the teapot with a shino glaze.

Soda-fired slab-built teapot, height: 16 cm (6¼ in.).

Cutting out a teapot pattern.

Applying slurry to a mitred join.

Compressing join.

Pushing teapot body onto its base.

Rolling base join.

Attaching spout.

Shaping handle.

Attaching handle.

Attaching knob to lid.

Finished teapot prior to firing.

Petra's sources of inspiration come from many things. She is attracted to objects which have been eroded by the elements or changed with time. Old buildings, rusty nails, crab claws found on the tide line, seed pods, etc. These form the beginning of an idea for Petra, as even the variety of shaped facets on her pots will effect how these inspired marks could be applied.

Petra will often refer back to the collection of marks on the newspaper sheets previously mentioned. Although now distant and distinct from their origin, they can provide unpredictable inspiration for the future.

Her teapots are once-fired to 1300°C (2372°F) in a wood kiln, with soda introduced to the kiln to provide a spontaneous and varied glazed surface. The positioning of the teapot in the kiln can greatly affect the end result; trial and error have determined the best spot to be on the top shelf.

Glaze Recipe
Shino glaze

Nepheline syenite	75
AT Ball clay	25

Cathi Jefferson (Canada)

Cathi works in Deep Cove, North Vancouver, making a range of wood-fired salt-glazed pottery. All her teapots are functional and she enjoys the thought of people using them. All her teapots are made on the wheel. She uses a porcellaneous stoneware body, called B-mix, from Laguna Clay in California, which has a warm tone that underlies and relates to the earthy colours she loves to work with.

The lid is the first part to be thrown and is off the hump, upside down with the knob on it. It is important to have a flange on the lid to enhance the fit, but also to help lower the lid's centre of

ABOVE AND INSET (DETAIL) *Wood-fired, salt-glazed teapot, height: 22.5 cm (9 in.).*

OPPOSITE PAGE

TOP AND BOTTOM *Front and back of a wood-fired, salt-glazed teapot, height: 22.5 cm (9 in.).*

Wood-fired, salt-glazed tea set.

gravity so that it is less likely to fall off when the tea is being poured. The body of the teapot is initially thrown as a cylinder, and at this stage it is altered to be square. The top is then folded inwards and the flange completed for the lid to sit on. A small lip is created at the top of the gallery to stop the salt fusing the lid to the body.

The spout is thrown in the usual manner and then immediately squared and bent forward whilst the clay is soft. This is then attached to the body whilst leatherhard. In order for the spout to relate to the body and the rest of the teapot (and not look too protruding), bending it forwards then back a bit at the tip really alters the shape and softens the form.

The handle is pulled and applied to the teapot, where it is pulled for a second time, the bottom end folded upwards and attached. In order for the teapot to be used regularly it must be easy to pick up – especially when full of hot tea.

As with all the other elements of the teapot, the foot must relate to, and enhance, the whole form. The foot elevates the teapot from the surface. To see how important this is, mask out the feet with paper and see how it dramatically alters the weight of the pot. Four balls of clay are added for the feet, pressed in and then padded so that they conform to the rest of the shape.

Decorating starts once the piece is biscuit fired. The teapot is initially dipped in a wash, which is allowed to dry, consisting of:

| Helmer kaolin | 50% |
| Nepheline syenite | 50% |

The design is then pencilled in so that it makes sense from side to side, or frame to frame. When you look out of a window or a door frame you know the image you see will carry on even if you cannot actually see it. Cathi wants the design to relate to the form and to draw the eye around the piece.

Cathi's challenge in her salt firing is to ensure that each side of the teapot is interesting, both visually and texturally. She explores a small pallet of earthy colours that seem to have endless possibilities for her. Oxides and/or stains are added to terra sigillata and brushed onto the surface. The dark outline is brushed on with a fine sable brush capable of making very fine, consistent lines. The last step is to glaze the interior with a shino glaze. The teapot is fired in her salt kiln, with the firing cycle as follows:

- Light reduction from cone 08 (455°C/1751°F)
- At cone 9 (1280°C/2336°F) she starts salting adding 3 parts salt and 2 parts baking soda (rolled up in a moistened newspaper) at 20-minute intervals over the next 1½ hrs
- Oxidised for the last 30–60 minutes

The beauty of salt firing is placing the pots in direct line of the salt, or behind other pots to create shadows. Cathi has certain spots in her kiln where she really likes to put teapots – generally high salt areas so that the teapot will have variation in colour, tone and texture. Placing the handles facing outwards, directly in the path of lots of salt, will hopefully produce teapots with handles that have wonderful textural qualities, enhancing the attraction of being held.

Sarah Dunstan (England)

Sarah lives and works in St Ives, which is the home of the Leach pottery. She finds her creative surroundings keep her constantly immersed in art and inspiration.

Sarah does not like to design or plan the finished teapot on paper, but would rather let it evolve. However, she is constantly drawing and collating ideas in her sketchbook (see p.65). This is the most

Slab-built stoneware teapots, height: 22.5 cm (9 in.). Photograph by Steve Tanner.

important part of her work, as Sarah does not regard her teapots as domestic ware (although they are made to pour) but as being more decorative – the ceramic equivalent of the family silver!

Sarah's teapots are slab-built in porcelain. She initially rolls out a thin slab of porcelain, at which stage most of the decoration is applied. This slab becomes her canvas. She draws onto the clay with finely extruded porcelain, impresses lace, or rolls the slab onto incised plaster batts.

To create the teapot, Sarah often uses a paper template to cut out the shape, like a pattern. She then constructs the slab into a cylinder form, to which a handbuilt spout and handle are added. Finally, she makes the lid to fit and complement the personality of the pot. To solve the problem of keeping the lid in place, Sarah has designed a long stopper, but it also fulfils an aesthetic issue – an element of surprise when you take the lid off!

The design process is a constant one – photographing, collecting and sketching images that she sees around her. Themes used to decorate her teapots also run through the rest of her work. The forms and

ABOVE *Lid with long stopper.* Photograph by Steve Tanner.
LEFT *Cylindrical form being decorated by impressing in the soft clay with a wooden tool.* Photograph by Steve Tanner.

textures of everyday metallic and material objects, such as baked bean and sardine tins, are an underlying inspiration for her work, together with fragmented architectural details such as chimney pots, railings, peeling paint and the lettering of painted signs. Living and working by the Cornish coast has its influences on Sarah's work; during walks on the beach she often picks up shells and sea-eroded glass or discovers interesting rock pools that have been the inspiration for her glazes with their precious glassy feel. Sarah also sees her finished teapots as having a very architectural feel, so as a group they may resemble a city skyline.

The finished piece is dried very slowly over several weeks to avoid splitting. It is bisque fired to 1000°C (1832°F). Sarah rubs cobalt carbonate into the details and glaze is applied using wax resist and dipping. Sarah usually fires with the lid in place, as it cannot stand by itself due to the stopper. Interestingly though, she doesn't use alumina or wadding but just prises it off very carefully! Sarah's teapots are small and light. They contain about two small cups of water. The handles are primarily aesthetically designed, but still functional.

Slab-built stoneware teapot, height: 22.5 cm (9 in.). Most of Sarah's teapots are fired to 1280°C (2336°F) in a small electric kiln, whereas her celadon teapots are reduction fired to 1280°C (2336°F) in a gas kiln.
Photograph by Steve Tanner.

Ray Bub (USA)

During the last ten years, Ray has been exploring the wheel-thrown hollow-ring form. The cross-sections of the ring range from round, square, triangular and pentagonal to oval. In a similar way to my work, Ray constructs his teapots by adding thrown ovoid bases, necks, lids, finials, spouts, and pulled handles.

Thrown ring vases can be found through various ages and cultures. An early example is an earthenware clay ring in the British Museum, dated to 340BC and made in the Apulia region of what is now south-eastern Italy. Other examples are:

- A 6th-century ring vase from the Kofun Dynasty, Japan
- Ring vases from the Tang, Song, and Ming Dynasties, China
- A 9th-century Moorish ring from Spain
- A 12th-century Persian ring vase
- An 18th-century American colonial ring-form pilgrim flask made in what is now New Jersey

More recently, he has been cutting the leatherhard hollow rings apart with a woodsman's bucksaw or an Exacto knife, then reassembling the separate arc sections into a pleasing composition using handbuilding methods. He then adds wheel-thrown and pulled elements to form a teapot. They are fired to cone 5 (1196°C/2185°F) in an electric kiln or cone 10 (1300°C/2372°F) in a propane-fired reduction kiln, and are functional. They make tea!

In the course of exploring new ideas, Ray often goes back to older ideas and reviews them in the light of what he has learned since making that earlier work. Since starting to cut apart and reassemble his wheel-thrown hollow rings, Ray has occasionally returned to his basic hollow-ring teapots.

This skinny large diameter ring has an elegant presence to which Ray was greatly attracted. Once completed and turned upright, it suggested the ring of fire that surrounds Shiva Nataraj, the dancing Shiva of the Hindu pantheon. Ray chose a satin gloss black glaze to further this impression of fire. The coiled finial on the lid continues the line of the coiled base, like an inverted tornado. In this artwork, Ray was looking at his original idea, without embellishments or alterations. It was fired to cone 10 (1300°C/2372°F) in reduction.

Ray describes this teapot as a breakthrough piece for him, as he assembled the teapot without joining any of the arc sections end-to-end. Furthermore, he decided to make it look as if he had broken the ring apart rather than cut it with a straight saw blade. To achieve this, Ray cut the ring into jagged edge sections with an Exacto knife, then filled in the open ends and textured them to look like the broken ends of sticks of wood. These were then assembled into the composition by joining most of the arc sections in their middles.

A base was constructed on three points. The handle and spout are on either side of the cut-open trapdoor lid. Ray did not add a finial to the lid, as the composition was already visually complex. Ray glazed the 'torn ends' with a glossy dark blue glaze, which was then sponged off so the ends were unglazed, except in the crevices where the dark blue glaze was caught. The whole teapot was then glazed in a matt blue-gold glaze. The torn ends were sponged off again to reveal the bare clay with the glossy dark blue glaze in the crevices. It was fired to cone 5 (1196°C/2185°F) in oxidation. This teapot composition has inspired all of Ray's subsequent work. He now reassembles the arc sections every which way without limiting himself to rejoining the sections end-to-end.

This teapot is more sculptural than functional, with room for only one cup of tea in the whole interior. The cross-section is a triangle with a large fin curving out from its top. Ray restated the ring cross-section with the triangular lid finial. For this teapot, Ray attaches the arc sections to each other

LEFT Jet Black Upright Ring
Teapot, *height: 38 cm (15 in.).*
BELOW LEFT Red Frost,
reassembled hollow-ring teapot,
height: 22.5 cm (9 in.).
RIGHT Grasshopper Leaping,
reassembled hollow-ring teapot,
height: 40 cm (16 in.).

Photographs by Jon Barber.

119

more than once. This results in a dense interlocking composition, with the middle arc section attached in three places to other arc sections.

After biscuiting, Ray glazed this with a matt tan glaze over a glossy dark green glaze, and fires it to cone 11 (1315°C/2399°F) in a reduction-fired gas kiln. It warped toward the flame somewhat, and he had to grind the base with a glass-grinding wheel.

Ray's inspiration for *Red Frost* came from a modernist architectural design element. The cantilever, or overhanging segment of a building, is attached vertically to a buried protruding 'foot'. With this teapot, Ray wants to preserve the circular form of the triangular ring. To achieve this, he cuts out only a small arc segment and then attaches it crosswise above its original place in the ring. Ray then orients the ring assembly almost horizontally on the oval base, which serves as the cantilever foot.

He sculpts the lid finial to mirror the cut-out arc segment, and attaches it to the lid, adding the handle and spout opposite each other in line with the oval base. Because of the fragility of the piece, Ray has to place a removable clay prop under the ring just below where the spout is attached during biscuit and glaze firing the teapot. After biscuiting, the pot is dipped into an opaque white glaze, then the pale green glaze is sponge-printed on all the edge features, and then the pink glaze poured over the whole teapot. Ray envisaged that this teapot would fire to a pink colour. However, due to worn out element wires in his electric kiln and the controller shutting off the kiln twice during the firing (resulting in the kiln being on 7 hours longer than the usual 12–14 hours needed to complete a cone 5 (1196°C/2185°F) firing), the normally pink glaze is transformed into a wonderful deep frosty red. Ray does not think this unusual glaze colour can be duplicated, but who knows, maybe the kiln god will surprise him!

You may also notice that the spout side of the ring curves almost a full inch above the handle side of the ring. The ring sags down on the right side of the removable prop, kicking up the end to the left of the spout because of the long hot soak time during the 21-hour firing. Ray likes this slight upward-spiral effect very much, although he did not plan it. A potential disaster can often lead to unexpected sources of inspiration!

With each reassembled hollow-ring teapot, Ray tries to incorporate something new. Here he makes the teapot ring in two parts, the first a wide shallow open ring 'tray' with a floor and two sides but no top. The second part is a wide flat ring measured to sit on the top edges of the ring-shaped open tray.

When both parts are leatherhard, Ray smears the edges with clay slip, and places the flat ring on top of the open tray ring. This creates a large flat closed ring with a trapezoidal cross-section. After pressing the seams together, Ray lets the assembly dry back to leatherhard. He then cuts the large hollow flat ring into three sections with zigzag ends. Ray seals up each open end and then reassembles the three ring segments into the upright composition. This is mounted on a thrown oval base, a spout made from clay slabs is added, and the handle is pulled. Ray then cuts the lid opening out of the section above the handle attachment.

After biscuiting, the teapot is glazed with a thin coat of pale green cone 5 (1196°C/2185°F) glaze. He then pours on a coat of the pink cone 5 glaze, and fires the teapot in the electric kiln to cone 5.

OPPOSITE
Bird of Paradise, *reassembled hollow-ring teapot, height: 45 cm (18 in.).* Photograph by Jon Barber.
INSET Sky Blue Torn Ends, *square cross-section reassembled hollow-ring teapot, height: 35 cm (14 in.).* Photograph by Jon Barber.

Making sequence

1 *Ray throwing the inner and outer walls of the hollow ring on the wheel.*

2 *Closing up the top of the hollow ring.*

3 *Ray at the potter's wheel holding the completed hollow ring.*

4 *Cutting the ring sections apart with a woodsman's bucksaw.*

5 *Sealing the cut-apart ring section with a clay slab cut to fit.*

6 *Adding the thrown spout to the completed leatherhard reassembled ring composition, which is mounted on a thrown oval base.*

7 *Pulling the handle on the completed leatherhard reassembled composition. The lid will subsequently be cut out of the ring section, and the 'Jackrabbit Leaping' lid finial added to complete the teapot.*

Richard Dewar (France)

Richard runs his pottery in France, where he makes a range of salt-glazed pots. Over the last 20 years Richard has produced over 200 different styles of teapot. He says that all of them work, even the dafter ones! The teapots are thrown using stoneware clay from St Amand-en-Puisaye, France. The teapot bodies are either thrown the right way up and then assembled in the usual manner, or they are thrown, then turned sideways, or upside down, and turned into a body shape for the other component parts to be added. Whichever way, the body must be strong enough in its own right to be able to withstand the quite outrageous spouts and handles to be attached.

For the slabbed teapots Richard adds fine grog to his standard throwing body as this helps to open up the clay and avoid any cracking during drying. The forms are generally quite flat – almost profiles of pots. Richard likes his teapots to be fairly humorous and happy-looking and therefore prefers the handle and especially the spout to stand proud. He applies a similar formula to his jugs.

His spouts are thrown and any twisting that occurs does not bother him a great deal as he says 'the pots are twisted as well'. However, he has noticed that

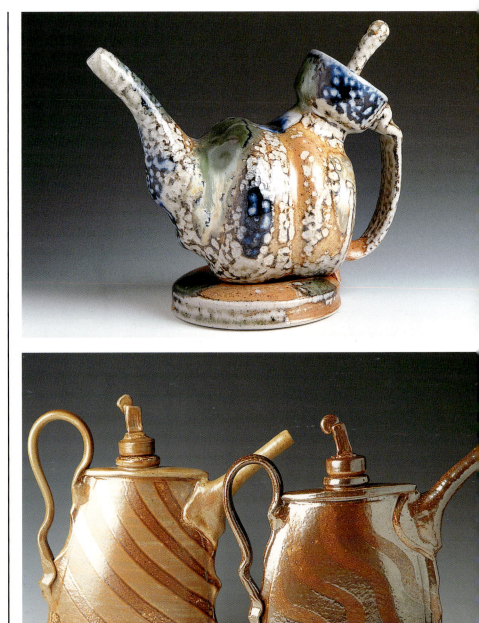

TOP *Salt-glazed 'Snail' teapot, height: 20 cm (8 in.). Thrown as an enclosed form then placed sideways on its thrown foot. Lid and handle are applied at leatherhard and decorated with coloured vitreous slips.* Photograph by Didier Rochefort.

ABOVE *Pair of flat salt-glazed teapots, height: 21cm (8¼ in.).* Photograph by Didier Rochefort.

ABOVE LEFT *Pair of barrel-shaped salt-glazed teapots, height: 21 cm (8¼ in.). Thrown body which, after turning, was placed on its side. Feet, lid and handle were applied at leatherhard and decorated with coloured vitreous slips.* Photograph by Didier Rochefort.

ABOVE RIGHT *Salt-glazed teapot, height: 21cm (8¼ in.). Thrown teapot with off-centre cut opening.* Photograph by Didier Rochefort.

spouts twist less when thrown on a kickwheel. To prevent the spout dribbling, Richard gives the freshly cut end a quick tap with a flat piece of wood, thus flattening the circular or oval end. This tends to push a small edge of clay inside the spout, which will act to cut the tea flow off abruptly. His handles are usually pulled and he likes them to be perky, giving additional character to his pieces.

He prefers, for his purely functional teapots, to have a gallery and a flange on the lid. Otherwise the lid and gallery can be more flexible. Richard's lids are small, even on quite large teapots, and he thinks of them as 'a little bit like the cherry on top of the cake'. The advantage of French teabags is that they all have a little string attached, thus facilitating the extraction of the bag from the teapot. This means that Richard can make his teapots with really quite minute lid openings in the knowledge that with the use of this thin string the teabag can be extracted relatively easily.

Teapots are generally quite complicated forms and Richard tends to decorate his quite freely. He dips, sprays, brushes and trails his slips and glazes. All Richard's pots are once-fired and he glazes the insides when the pots are leatherhard. All outer decoration is carried out when the pots are bone dry. The pots are salt fired to cone 11 (1315°C/2399°F), with a 5-hour reduction and a 2-hour salting. The more salt effect he requires on any given piece, the more closely it has to be placed to the firebox. If he wants a gentler effect, he hides the pot behind others in the kiln.

Richard's teapots have a great feeling of fun and laughter. When I made this comment to him he explained that when he makes his teapots he is smiling or laughing. Similarly, when someone looks at the finished piece they usually smile too!

Glaze Recipe

Basic slip

China clay	50
Powdered bone china	50

Vitreous slip

Nepheline syenite	33
China clay	33
Ball clay	33

Making sequence

1 *Richard coiling the base of the enormous teapot.*
2 *The coiling continues upwards to the shoulder then inwards to the gallery.*
3 *Richard attaching the knob onto the handle. The lid was thrown and its knob created from a textured coil of clay.*
4 *Due to its size, Richard created the spout from two pieces, here he attaches the second part.*
5 *Richard adding the handle which was first stretch-pulled flat on the table using a damp sponge.*
6 *Finished unfired teapot.*

Richard Godfrey (England)

Richard makes a wonderful variety of funky teapots, which he often describes as three-dimensional jazz. He lives by the coast and is continually inspired by contrasts in the environment.

Bi-valve teapot

Richard creates the body of his *Bi-valve Teapot* using a technique which he calls 'slumped slabbing'. As in nature, the bi-valve is comprised of two halves, and Richard makes the teapot body in two halves.

Slabs are cut from a block of clay using two notched sticks and a wire. These slabs are a touch thicker than required and are put through a slab roller to compress them and reduce the thickness a little. The triangular shape of the bi-valve body is drawn onto the base of a cardboard box (a banana box from the supermarket in this case) and cut out with a sharp knife. The slabbed clay is then draped over the hole in the box. Lifting the box 8 cm (3 in.) off the bench, Richard drops it, the clay slumping into the hole. Using a rubber kidney Richard refines the shape, swelling out the form.

To ensure that both halves of the bi-valve share the same contour, he uses a simple stick guide to gauge the profile. The clay is

Bi-valve Teapot, *height: 23 cm (9 in.).*

allowed to firm up at this stage before the surplus clay is cut away. The first half of the bi-valve is then kept moist, wrapped in plastic. The second half of the bi-valve is created in the same way. Richards uses the stick guide to ensure that the profiles are similar, and because they are made from the same initial shape in the box they will fit together. The two halves are then joined together with slip.

The edges of the teapot body are an important feature in the overall design and look of the teapot. Richard therefore spends some considerable time forming and sharpening these edges. He uses a wooden stick to carefully beat the edges at the corners. Final forming and smoothing is done with a plastic phonecard or

metal kidney. Richard then builds the cradle type base from extruded hollow coils and mounts the teapot body within it.

The handle is made from several extruded coils joined together, and attached to the body when firm. The teapot spout is made from similar extruded coils; two of these are attached to the body and a hole is drilled through each. These two spouts emit two lovely jets of tea. At this stage other decorative details such as the 'exhaust pipes' are added. Richard completes the teapot by cutting the lid directly into the teapot body using a scalpel. He then adds two little buttons to act as locators for the lid. The completed teapot is allowed to dry out straightaway and is decorated when bone dry.

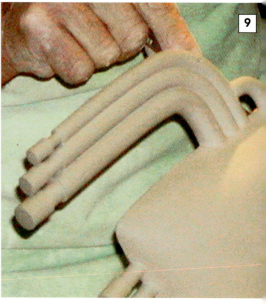

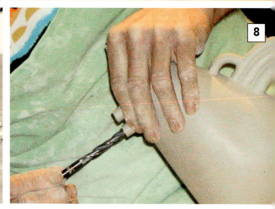

Making sequence

1 Slabbed clay slumped in the mould.
2 Cleaning up the edge prior to joining.
3 Carefully joining the two halves.
4 Cleaning up the edges of the form using a metal kidney.
5 Assembling the handle made from extruded coils.
6 Mounting the teapot body on the cradle.
7 Attaching the handle to the teapot body.
8 Drilling out the spouts.
9 Cutting the lid directly into the teapot body using a scalpel.
10 The finished teapot.

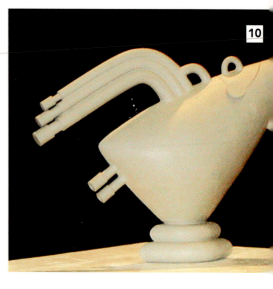

Rocket Dogfish Teapot

Richard uses more traditional construction techniques for his *Rocket Dogfish Teapot*. He draws freehand the outline of the teapot body on the two slabs of clay, laid one on top of the other. Using a sharp knife he cuts the two identical sides of the teapot body, and chamfers each of the sides, using a wire with a 30°, 45° or 60° angle, depending on the join. Each slab is then gently curved using a rubber kidney before being joined together. To prevent sagging of the form, Richard speed-dries these slabs using a flame torch. A third slab and a base are added.

Finally, legs and handle are added. Once dry, Richard decorates it with coloured slips that are sprayed on, masking out certain areas. He adds up to 25% of commercial stain and uses a variety of fluxes, especially calcium borate

frit and lead bisilicate, to achieve his vivid colours. More detailed decoration is applied with brushes and sponges. The pieces are biscuited before being finally dipped in a clear glaze and fired to 1140°C (2084°F).

Making sequence

1 *The two slabs.*
2 *Chamfering the edges.*
3 *Speed-drying to aid handling and prevent sagging.*
4 *A third slab is added.*
5 *Viewed from the other side.*
6 *Adding final slab.*

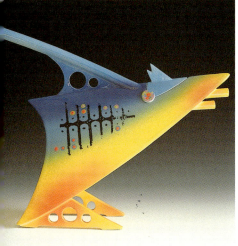

Rocket Dogfish Teapot, *height: 30 cm (12 in.).*

ABOVE Fenix Teapot, *height:
23 cm (9 in.).*
ABOVE RIGHT Chick Teapot,
height: 23 cm (9 in.).
RIGHT Red Cockerel Teapot,
height: 23 cm (9 in.).

Glaze Recipe

*Clear glaze,
1120°C–1140°C/2048°F–2084°F)
with 15 minute soak at top
temperature*

Lead bisilicate frit	65
Calcium borate frit	10
Potash feldspar	10
China clay	8
Flint	5
Whiting	2

Richard Wilson (England)

Richard makes a wide range of domestic earthenware, including a variety of functional teapots, with each piece having a sense of personality. Richard's underlying influences stem from English and east European folk ceramics that were made purely to be used and occasionally decorated for beauty. 'There is a wonderful sculptural process involved in the assembly and making of a teapot, with four individual pieces that go together to create one overall form.'

Richard throws the teapot body on a batt, whereas the lid and spout are thrown off the hump. The next day when the clay is firm he turns the foot-ring, cuts the holes for the sieve, and attaches the spout. The handle is pulled from the body. To enhance the form and give each piece more character, Richard often lifts the teapot body with a foot-ring or three small feet. On some teapots Richard flutes the spouts with a cheese-cutter to exaggerate the form of the spout, making them just a little more individual.

When building the teapot, Richard is careful to consider the relationships between all the four aspects of the teapot: body, spout, handle and lid. He believes a source of balance and proportion between them is important, especially the top of the spout and handle, which should be in alignment.

The constructed teapot is placed upside down to dry before being dipped in white slip. When leatherhard, the teapots are decorated in keeping with the themes that run throughout his work, but he always considers his teapots as individuals and decorates them accordingly. Richard decorates his pots using slips. Initially, everything is dipped in a white slip and when this is almost dry he applies the coloured slips. His decorating involves large brushes that are swept across the surface in broad sweeping motions to maintain the vitality in the brushstroke. The secret in getting the vibrancy and life into the brushstroke is to apply the

TOP *Earthenware teapot, height: 22.5 cm (9 in.).*
BOTTOM *Earthenware teapot, height: 22.5 cm (9 in.).*

decoration with speed and confidence. Any hesitation is instantly recognised. Further decoration is added using slip trailers.

The pots are biscuit fired then glaze fired in oxidation to a very soft cone 3 (1170°C/2138°F). His lids are fired separately as both rims are glazed.

Roger Cockram (England)

In recent years, Roger's ceramics have been influenced by the broad theme of 'natural water'. His pots reflect the colours, rhythms and sense of spiraling movement often observed in this environment. This has led to studying the animals which inhabit this world, but he is only interested in using animals in the context of form and surface. Roger finds the teapot form has many opportunities for variation and humour, and has recently developed a group of teapots based on fishes, frogs and newts. His finished pieces are intended to make the viewer smile.

Roger's designs require a great deal of thought and preparation, incorporating a mixture of rough models and quick sketches, plus 'learning from the piece itself' as it progresses. The pots are firstly thrown then modelled and sponged, brushed with glazes and vitreous slips. All are then once-fired to cone 11 (1315°C/2399°F) in a reduction atmosphere.

The body of the pot is thrown with soft clay and is left to dry to soft leatherhard. It has to be stiffened enough to take the modelling of the handle and spout without deformation. The clay used for modelling a fish handle, for example, is of a different recipe from that of the body. Roger has chosen

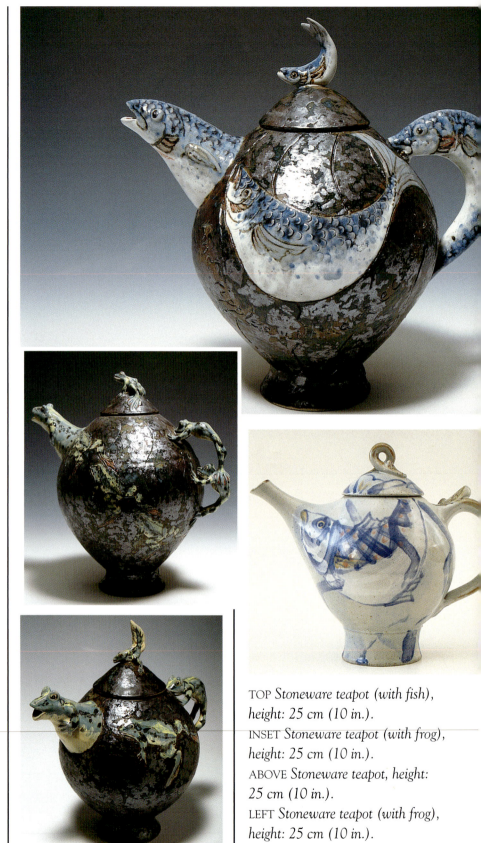

TOP *Stoneware teapot (with fish), height: 25 cm (10 in.).*
INSET *Stoneware teapot (with frog), height: 25 cm (10 in.).*
ABOVE *Stoneware teapot, height: 25 cm (10 in.).*
LEFT *Stoneware teapot (with frog), height: 25 cm (10 in.).*

Making sequence

1 *Roger modelling the fine detail of the frog spout. He uses a variety of modelling tools, mostly homemade.*
2 *Roger modelling the fine detail of the frog handle.*
3 *An outline of the decoration for the teapot body is marked onto the surface with a sharp tool.*
4 *Finishing the modelling of the small fish on the lid.*
5 *The pot decoration almost complete, Roger finishes sponging the background slips onto the raw clay. Note that the fish motifs have been protected from this slip by waxing.*

his modelling clays for their shrinkage values, in order to match that of the body (which has already shrunk to leatherhard). Were it to be the same recipe, it would be likely to shrink more and crack off at the drying or firing stages. Therefore Roger uses clay with a lower shrinkage rate than that of the throwing clay, thereby solving the problem. All the modelling is done by hand. Roger is not interested in moulds, but rather in achieving an appropriate shape and proportion for the size and shape of the teapot body beneath. The 'fish' teapot, for example, is meant to depict a wave flowing through the pot. The handle flows through to the fish on the side and finally to the modelled spout. This spout is suggestive of a ship's figurehead.

The pot is covered and left to dry slowly before being decorated when completely dry. For this, Roger uses a range of different glazes, either painted or dotted onto the surface, so that the different colours blend into one another during firing. The background colour of the body is intended to be more matt than the painted 'wet' fish or frog, and for this he uses sponged layers of vitreous slips. These have sufficient flux in them to ensure partial vitrification but not so much as to fully melt like the glaze used on the animals themselves. The colours and tones for the fish are derived from drawings over many years. All the glazes are designed to shrink at the same rate as the pot.

The firing is all done in one process. Roger has never biscuit fired a pot in 27 years and really does not see the point. His technique is quite simple: the temperature is raised quite slowly for some hours, then, when red hot, the rate is increased. At about 1000°C (1832°F), he commences reduction and the kiln proceeds up to 'cone 11 bending' (1315°C/ 2399°F). At this point he turns it off and rapid cools it for an hour before closing everything down. In other words, Roger raw fires; he does a biscuit firing and then just keeps on going.

Sandy Lockwood (Australia)

Sandy lives and works in NSW, Australia. She makes a wide range of wood-fired, salt-glazed domestic ware. In her kitchen, Sandy has a range of different teas that she uses on a regular basis: ordinary household, Chinese black, Japanese and herbal. For each type of tea she selects an appropriate teapot, which matches both tea and occasion. She believes that this makes a difference to one's enjoyment of the beverage.

This intimate association with the use of the teapot is the foundation of her making. Sandy's attitude to tea drinking is one of the greatest motivations for her designs. She tries to make teapots that not only enhance the process of making tea but which also stand alone as objects of aesthetic merit. Her teapots are not separate from her other work; rather they are an extension to another aspect of her basic philosophy in relation to clay.

Sandy believes that clay has a softness and responsiveness that is very seductive in nature and she aims to maintain a freshness and spontaneity in her work, capturing a moment in time which can be seen in the completed piece. The decoration of Sandy's pots comes mainly from the wood-fired salt kiln, though some minimal decoration – such as throwing lines, edge detail or small impressions in soft clay – are added at the wheel. The salt-glazing process hides nothing – it has a nakedness and simplicity that speaks directly to the viewer.

The first stage is to throw the teapot body, lid and spout as normal. Sandy usually makes the lid with a flange that sits well down inside the pot and is slightly longer than normal. This reduces the risk of it falling out. When the teapot body is leatherhard, the interior is raw glazed with a shino type glaze (see recipe opposite). After applying the glaze and once the body has firmed up, Sandy makes strainer holes and trims the end of the spout. Sometimes, having cut the end of the spout at the angle required, she pulls a little lip at the bottom edge.

Wood-fired, salt-glazed porcelain teapot, height: 22.5 cm (9 in.).

Sandy used to use cane or wooden handles, but she now prefers to make her own, as she believes they become a more integral part of the pot. Part of the character of her teapot comes from the relationship of the spout and handle, creating an impression of lightness.

Once the pot is bone dry, the outside is either sprayed with glaze or slip. However, many pots have no external slip or glaze, but are decorated by the salt-glazing and wood-firing process, which is the final and key stage in the making process. Teapots are placed in a number of different spots in the kiln to produce a variety of effects created by the flame, ash and salt. Usually, Sandy points the spout towards the flame, because if the teapot is placed sideways there is a risk that the spout will bend towards the flame. The path of the flame, amount of salt vapour present, and temperature variations along the length of the kiln, all produce variety in the colour and texture of each piece. As a result, each piece of salt-glazed work is unique, a key factor in making this style so special.

ABOVE LEFT *Wood-fired, salt-glazed porcelain teapot, height: 22.5 cm (9 in.).*

ABOVE *Wood-fired, salt-glazed porcelain teapot thrown then altered, height: 22.5 cm (9 in.).*

LEFT *Wood-fired, salt-glazed porcelain teapot, height: 22.5 cm (9 in.).*

Glaze Recipe

Shino glaze

Nepheline syenite	80
Ball clay	20

Sheila Casson (England)

Sheila worked with her late husband Mick in Upton Bishop. Whereas Mick's teapots convey an image of strength and solidity, Sheila's teapots have a light, feminine image.

Sheila first throws the body of her teapots, making them in batches of five. The body is thrown without a base, the gallery edge is compressed and thickened for strength and a line scribed round the rim to emphasise the edge. A small amount of water is placed on the wheel-head inside and out. The pot is then wired through so that it floats on the film of water. Four points are marked out and knuckled in to create the flowing four-star shape. The water is then removed and the pot put to one side to dry while the lid is thrown.

Once the body has dried to soft leatherhard, a base is rolled out which is slightly larger than required. The bottom edge of the teapot body is then scored and slurry applied; this is then placed onto the slab (note: the base is not scored). The base is then cut round the shape of the skirted body leaving roughly 5 mm (¼ in.) extra. This excess clay is then beaten with a flat piece of wood to create the 'hem' of the skirt. This process naturally creates an irregular 'hem', which Sheila likes.

The standard teapot spout has a slight bulge at its base where it joins the pot. However, Sheila does not want this 'pout' under her spout as it interferes with the delicate line of her teapot. So, the spout is thrown off the hump and left on a board just until the clay has lost its sticky feel and is very soft leatherhard. Meanwhile Sheila uses an old dry spout to act as a template to mark the position of the spout. The spout and handle will spring from the teapot body at the same height, reinforcing the symmetry within the piece. The sieve holes are then cut.

The base of the thrown spout is then cut, scored and slurried, and attached to the teapot body. Because the spout is very soft and malleable, Sheila can smooth away the 'pout' and create a smooth curve from the foot of the teapot to the end of the spout.

Pursuing the light feminine image of Sheila's teapot, the handle has by definition to be light and delicate. Sheila's handle is round in cross-section, slowly tapering from top to bottom as would the arm. Pulling the handle gently from all sides creates a round handle that gently and gracefully tapers, this is then arched into shape and left to firm up. Once firm, the bottom edge of the handle is cut so that the handle goes straight onto the body. Both surfaces are scored and slurried and then pressed together. This is a difficult process to master to keep the lines smooth and strong. Sheila's tip is, 'don't clean up the surface or slurry too soon. Let the handle joint firm up then cut away the excess slurry, etc. This allows you to keep the edges sharp and clean.'

The teapot is left to dry slowly. After biscuiting the teapot is glazed inside, and Sheila blows down the spout to clear the sieve of glaze. A blue slip is applied to the outside of the teapot. Finally the piece is fired in the workshop's salt kiln

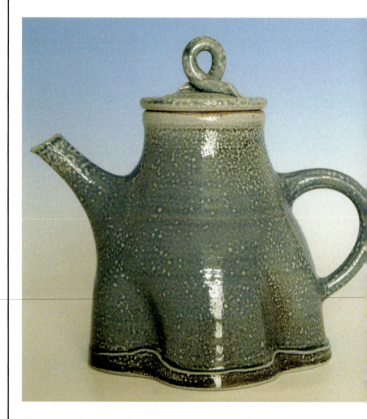

Salt-glazed teapot, height: 22.5 cm (9 in.).

John Jelfs (England)

John's pots are designed primarily to be used, and over the years he has concluded that the better they look, the better they perform. John believes that teapot making is a real challenge because the individually made components have to work as a whole.

He usually makes a dozen pots at a time, ranging in size from 1 pint (0.57 litres) up to 1 gallon (4.6 litres). They are all hand-thrown, with the spouts coming from a single hump of clay. The body is altered whilst still damp (fluted, impressed, creased or ovalled) before assembly commences.

John thinks it is important that the pot feels balanced in the hand, i.e. the handle must be large enough to accommodate the fingers and keep them away from the heat of the pot, but at the same time not be too large and thus create a strain on the wrist. His pots are thinly thrown, partly to avoid excessive weight, but also to prevent the tea from losing its heat. He also likes his pots to pour without the lid falling off, and they mustn't drip.

The majority of John's pots are wood-ash glazed, the rest have a white feldspathic or tenmoku glaze. He flutes the sides of many of his teapots. The secret is to get comfortable and to be able to hold the pot securely and sturdily. Remember not to grip too hard and be careful not to distort the gallery. Holding the tool firmly and with a single sweeping stroke of his arm, John cuts a clean swathe from top to bottom. Notice how the tool is cutting the clay, creating a 5 cm (2 in.) piece of swarf. This happens when the clay is in the right condition – firm leatherhard. As with turning, if the clay is too soft the tool will plough the surface. If it's too hard then it will only scratch the surface and you will have to repeat the process several times, losing that crispness, and giving the impression that it has been messed around with and laboured. As with most things in life, this technique takes time to master.

The pots are biscuited and then glazed with a dry wood ash ochre glaze (high alumina) and fired in a gas

TOP *Stoneware teapot, height: 20cm (8 in.).*
ABOVE *John fluting the side of his teapot with a tool made from a hacksaw blade.*

kiln with reduction from 1000°C (1832°F) onwards for 6 hours until reaching top temperature of cone 10. John achieves his unique matt glazes by not having a typical oxidizing purge at top temperature, allowing the kiln to cool slowly (no crash cool).

Steve Harrison (England)

The traditional method of creating an octagonal pot, handed down from early Chinese porcelain potters, was to throw a thick walled vessel and cut away the facets with a wire. Steve's design could have been achieved this way but it would not have given him the accuracy of the facets or the lightness of the teapot body.

Therefore, Steve constructed a mould with a space at the top and bottom. This allows the foot and gallery to be thrown differently each time. This contradicts the stereotypical use of a mould and creates an innovative way of making pots.

THIS PAGE
ABOVE *Stoneware teapot, height: 20cm (8 in.).*
BELOW *Stoneware teapot, height: 20cm (8 in.).*

OPPOSITE PAGE
TOP *Blue salt-glazed octagonal teapots, height: 22.5 cm (9 in.).*

Making sequence

1 *The mould is placed over a freshly thrown cylinder. The wall thickness is generous to allow it to be thrown into the mould.*
2 *The cylinder is very slowly thrown into the facets of the mould – it has to be done in a few stages, allowing it to touch the mould on the final pull. A coil of clay is now added to throw the top of the pot. It is easier to add a coil rather than throw clay that was in the cylinder.*
3 *After a period of 30 minutes the mould can be split and the body of the teapot revealed.*
4 *The teapot is finished with a pressed spout and handle.*

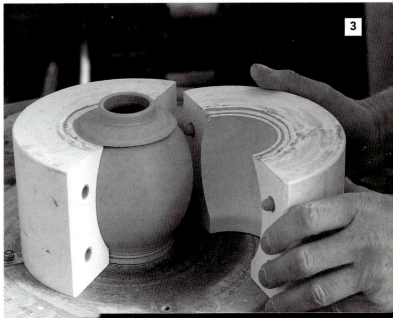

1

3

2

4

Steve Woodhead (England)

I enjoy the improvisation of form and structure through making a wide range of individual teapots.

My work features textured surfaces over which coloured glazes flow. The interaction of the glazes with the textured surfaces creates unique qualities, which have become characteristic of my work. I use porcelain, as the whiteness of the clay does not 'muddy' the colours.

'Oriental' Teapot

The *'Oriental' Teapot* is thrown in porcelain on the wheel. I make the gallery slightly thicker than usual for stability, as the handle has a tendency to pull it into an oval. At the final stage of throwing I turn the wheel slowly, and carve a deep spiral into the side of the body using a metal rib.

'Oriental' Teapot, *height: 25cm (10 in.), porcelain.*

TOP *Pressing a coil of clay into the textured surface.*
ABOVE *Throwing the coil onto a batt to flatten it.*

This spiral continues the sense of movement from the wheel.

The handle is made from coils of clay rolled onto a textured surface. A piece of sponge is used to press the clay onto the textured surface to avoid distorting the freshly pressed clay. One side of the coil is then repeatedly thrown onto a board to flatten it. This process results in a broad, flat handle with the beautifully textured surface on top. The handle is then slumped over a biscuited pot to give it a smooth, uniform curve. The handle supports are made in a similar way, being curved to reflect the shape of the teapot body.

Once soft leatherhard, the handle and spout are added, followed by the three feet, which are again made from textured coils of clay. I find it important to stand back at this stage and view the entire teapot from a distance. The shape of the handle is crucial to the final image.

Hollow Ring Teapot

This is a fun piece based on a 15th-century vase.

The hollow ring is thrown on the wheel. When leatherhard, it is turned and concentric circles are cut into the body to continue the circular theme. The ring is then mounted on a base and a spout and lid attached. The circular handles are thrown and grooved on both sides.

TOP Hollow Ring Teapot, *height: 25 cm (10 in.).*
ABOVE Rock 'n' Roll, *sculptural teapot, height: 12.5 cm (5 in.). This teapot is based upon 'Heart without a soul' but is considerably smaller, sitting on two flat feet. The teapot has a tendency to rock backwards and forwards, hence its title.*

'Bamboo' handle Teapot

Porcelain 'Bamboo' handle teapot (25 cm/10 in. high) by Steve Woodhead, Warwickshire, England.

1 When the two halves of the body are soft leatherhard I take the top half and turn the gallery.

2 The lid is turned to fit the gallery, ensuring a good, snug fit.

3 The edges are scored, slurried and joined together. I spend a little time compressing this joint together by gripping the edge as the pot rotates – effectively throwing it together. Using a turning tool, I turn the edge profile and make a feature of it.

4 Using a grooved cutter from a pencil sharpener, I create a textured edge to the teapot body. This cutter compresses the clay as it cuts, helping to create a good strong joint.

5 The spout is added.

6 Offering the handle up to the body to establish the length of the supporting rods.

7 Adding the two 'A' frames. The angle of the slope is crucial to the overall image of the teapot.

8 The handle is fixed to the two 'A' frames. The lid knob is added, using the same method of construction as the handle. The edges are curved upwards to create a feeling of movement and continuity.

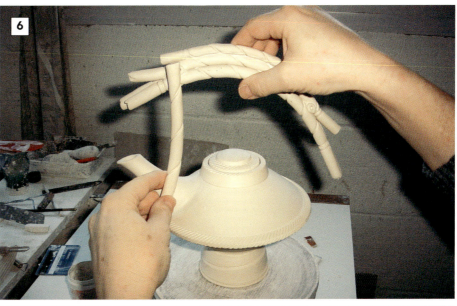

6

7

8

RIGHT 'Bamboo' handle teapot, *height: 20 cm (8 in.), the body is based on a more traditional form.*
BELOW Bulbous Teapot, *height: 25 cm (10 in.).*
BOTTOM Heart Without a Soul, *sculptural teapot, height: 20 cm (8 in.). This piece has the heart of a teapot, consisting of all the correct parts, but because the body has no base it cannot hold any liquid and therefore has no soul.*

Steven Hill (USA)

Steven makes his teapots to be functional and they are meant to be used, but at the same time he wants them to have sculptural presence. So like many things in life, he has to balance the requirements of these two seemingly disparate criteria.

According to Steven, some of the pots he makes seem to just flow off his fingers, such as bowls, plates, mugs, and vases. Teapots, on the other hand, bring out the side of him that gets caught up in details. How large should the diameter of the spout be and how do the angle and length influence pouring? Or how can I put a spiral in my spout without adversely affecting its ability to pour? Or how can I design a successful locking device for the lid? Or how can I make a teapot that is sculpturally appealing without impairing its functionality?

Stephen feels that teapots are tedious to assemble, so he usually makes them in a small group of four to eight at a time. He gets involved in solving the various technical and aesthetic problems that arise and before he knows it two days are gone! After making a group of teapots he usually likes to relax by making a series of simpler forms such as bowls or mugs.

Steven's earliest teapots had English bamboo handles. They were quite functional, but in the end he wanted something more personal and began making the handles out of clay. Pulled handles arch over the top of his teapots, making them distinctively different from other pots he makes, and giving them a more sculptural profile. For many years he extruded and twisted his handles, but he has come to prefer the simplicity of a pulled handle.

Steven's spouts have been influenced by a story Peter Pinnell tells about how Chinese potters want their tea to pour '6 inches round'. To achieve this, the diameter must be small enough so that the tea fills the spout and so the stream doesn't break up for 6 inches (15 cm) or more after leaving the spout. This also demands that the narrowest part of the constriction be right at the tip of the spout so the tea doesn't fan out as it's being poured.

Most of his teapots have overhanging lids, with an

Stoneware teapot, height: 35 cm (14 in.). Extruded handle, slip trailed, sprayed multiple glazes, single-fired stoneware. Photograph by Al Surratt.

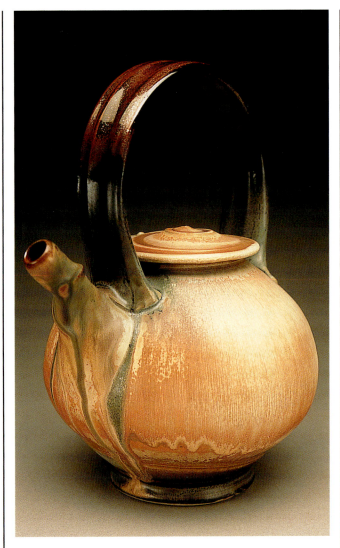

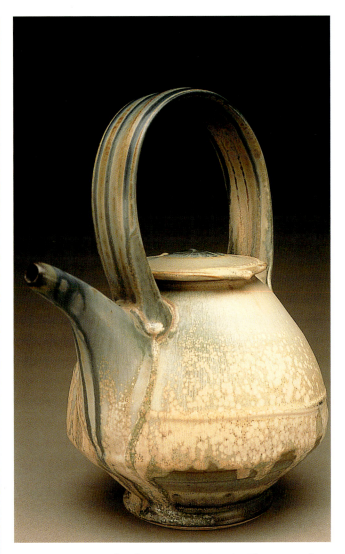

Stoneware teapot, height: 30 cm (12 in.). Thrown and altered, pulled handle, sprayed multiple glazes, single-fired stoneware.

Stoneware teapot, height: 30 cm (12 in.). Thrown and altered, pulled handle, ribbed surface design, single-fired stoneware.

interior flange and locking device. A half turn will keep the lid securely in place whilst pouring, and the overhanging edge allows the lid to be picked up easily without a knob. Steven feels that the simple uncluttered line of this type of lid complements his forms and surfaces.

Steven intends his teapots to be used, but realises they are generous in size. For him, the smaller the teapot the more troublesome it is to make. Whilst they might be too big for one or two people, hopefully they are just right for serving tea at a small dinner party. And making them a little larger does give them just a bit more of that elusive sculptural presence.

Making sequence

1 Steven starts by throwing a bulbous form, then expands the low waistline into the form using a metal rib. Using a trimming tool he defines the relationship between the foot and the lower belly. The corner of a metal rib is used to add a spiral movement to the underbelly of the form.

2 Applying a thick slip (as thick as possible) made from the throwing body to the upper two thirds of the freshly thrown form.

3 A very soft rubber rib is lightly run over the freshly slipped form, hoping to cause the slip to slump and drip in a sensuous manner. Sometimes he has to apply more slip and repeat the process several times before the slip falls the way he wants.

4 As the pot is turning on the wheel, Steven torches the inside of the form to keep it from collapsing because of the extra water absorbed from the thick slip.

5 The lid is thrown in the normal way, with Steven taking extra care to ensure that the calliper measurement is accurate.

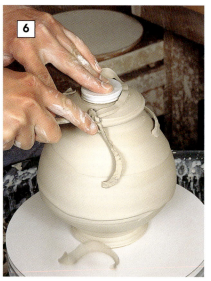

6 Steven trims the lid whilst in situ on the leatherhard body, holding it in place with a plastic bottle top.

7 He then applies slip to the lid and creates the pattern with the edge of the rubber rib.

8 Indentations are made with a paddle in the foot to liven up the link between the bottom of the pot and the table it rests on.

9 Throwing the spout off the hump. The spiral is formed by carefully drawing the rounded edge of the metal rib up the spout as it spins. Too much pressure and the spout twists off, too little and the mark is safe and predictable. If the spiral is too deep, he risks it interfering with the pouring.

10 The edge is smoothed with a chamois and then the spout is bent in preparation for attaching to the body.

11 The spout is cut in preparation for attachment to the body.

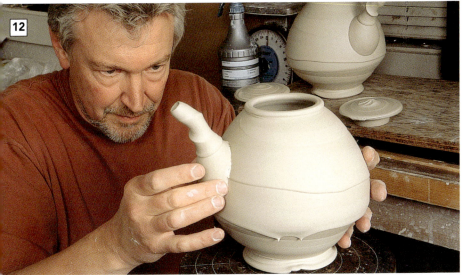

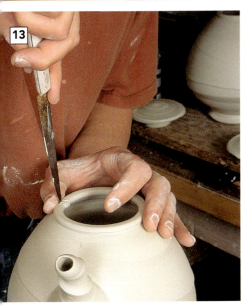

12 Strainer holes are cut in the body and the spout is attached.

13 Cutting a notch in the rim so that the lid (with locking device) will fit in.

14 Adding balls of clay which will act as a locking device.

15 Adding a key so that the user can easily identify where the locking lugs fit in.

16 Pulling a handle. For this type of handle, Steven needs one that gets larger at each end, for a butt attachment on each side of the lid. As he is pulling the handle, he gradually increases his pressure and then releases it again to leave extra clay at the handle ends.

17 Torching the handle a little so that it will hold its shape as it is arched over the pot.

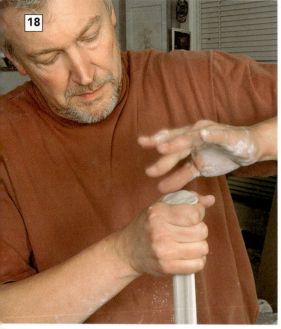

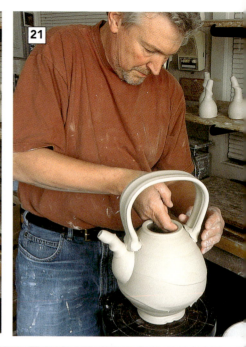

18 Patting the flange into the end of the handle for attachment.

19 Preparing to arch the handle over the teapot.

20 Arching the handle over the teapot.

21 Steven spends a lot of time refining the point of attachment and making sure that the handle arches gracefully over the pot. He does not want a symmetrical arch, but one that captures some tension in its curve.

22 Adding a small coil of clay to the inner join, smoothing in to create a continuous flow.

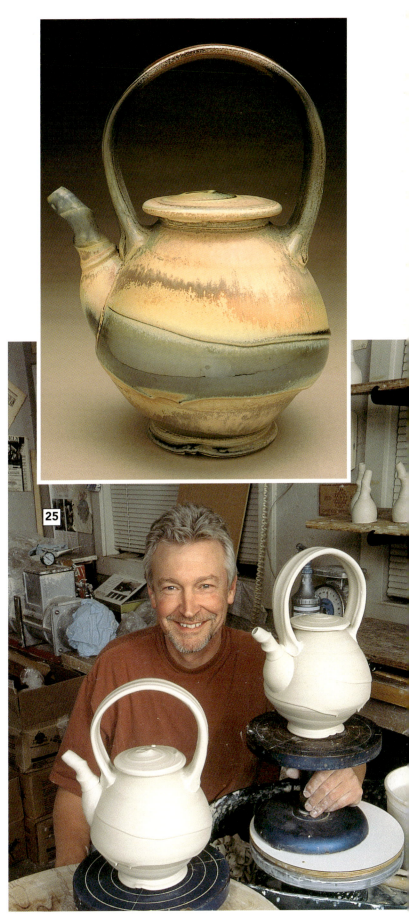

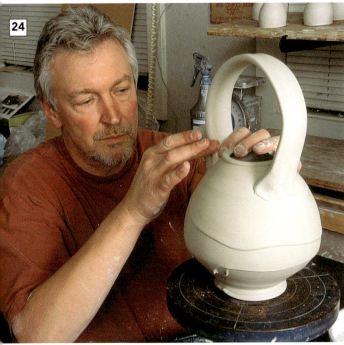

23 *Pushing the base of the handle into the shoulder with two thumb marks.*

24 *Steven finishing off the handle.*

25 *Completed teapots.*

ABOVE, INSET *Fired and glazed teapot.*

5 Gallery

THIS CHAPTER includes a gallery of teapots, most with a brief description of how it was made, exploring the wide diversity of studio potters today.

1

1 *Reduced stoneware teapot, height: 18 cm (7 in.) by* **Andrew & Joanna Young**, *Norwich, England.*

The teapot body and lid are thrown on the wheel and the lid is turned, whereas the handle is pulled and the spout is press-moulded. The teapot is assembled when leatherhard. Andrew and Joanna use a variety of roulettes, carved from a plaster mould, which are rolled over the leatherhard body. In this instance, the teapot body has been rouletted up and down vertically. A sprig, also made from a mould, has been used to apply a flower motif.

They raw fire their work so the teapot is glazed on the inside with a light shiny white glaze when the clay is semi-dry. It is then left to dry out completely before being dipped on the outside with a chromium glaze. A cobalt glaze is dabbed over this to highlight certain areas of the pot. Lastly, the teapot is raw glazed to 1320°C (2408°F) in a reduction kiln.

2 *Earthenware teapot, height: 38 cm (15 in.). by* **Alvin F Irving**, *Lancashire, England.* Photograph by Malcolm Farrer.

Alvin works predominantly in thrown white earthenware with some occasional slab work. He specialises in underglaze decoration, where all the decoration is brushwork – he does not use stencils, transfers or stamps. Handles and legs are either pulled or rolled, with sculptural features hand modelled.

Alvin concentrates on pieces which combine allegorical and commemorative images painted on

153

them. This teapot illustrates the return of recycled nuclear waste to Japan in 2001, which was subsequently sent back to Britain as it had not been processed as originally claimed. The base of this teapot bears the following inscription: 'Truth and justice lie on the grass, dogs piss where they like'. Despite its ornate appearance, this is a functional teapot that pours well!

3 *Soda-fired porcelain teapot, height: 15 cm (6 in.) by* **Jack Doherty**, *Herefordshire, England.* The teapot, lid and spout are thrown using Harry Fraser porcelain. The circular imprints are made immediately after the throwing, using a small piece of shaped wood. Jack works directly with the clay, trying to make each mark on the surface alter the form in a way which shows the softness of the clay.

When the pot is dry, the indentations are filled with a thin wash of copper carbonate and water. All Jack's work is once-fired and soda glazed. He mixes 2 kg (4.4 lb) of sodium bicarbonate with hot water and sprays this mixture into the kiln when the temperature reaches 1260°C (2300°F). The kiln is then fired to 1300°C (2372°F). The vaporising sodium reacts with the porcelain clay and copper carbonate, producing a subtle range of colour and surface quality.

4 *Porcelain teapot, height: 22.5 cm (9 in.), by* **Gail Russell**, *Ohio, USA.*
Gail works with Tom Turner at

their Peachblow pottery in Ohio, USA. She works predominantly with functional forms, being influenced by Oriental and Classical shapes. Her glazes also reflect these influences – copper reds, celadons and iron saturated glazes.

Colour variations are achieved by brushing a thin layer of her black glaze over the copper red, then brushing a linear design of an iron oxide and rutile wash over that, and finally, a trailing of white glaze. This layering creates a rainbow of colour and depth. Sometimes golden crystals will form where the iron and rutile wash is thick.

5 *Salt-fired porcelain teapot, height: 25cm (10 in.), thrown and reconstructed by* **Bruce Cochrane**, *Mississauga, Canada.* Photograph by Peter Hogan.
Bruce throws a slightly conical, bottomless cylinder, which is altered and paddled into a diamond-shaped form. The slab bottom and shoulder are attached. Thrown moulding is applied to the cut lip as a finishing detail. It is also used to outline the lid which is cut from the slab shoulder. The slab spout is formed around a cone-shaped wooden mould. The handle is pulled and flattened with a rib. The strap of clay around the base of the pot is a thrown element.

6 *Salt-fired porcelain teapot, height: 25 cm (10 in.), thrown, press-moulded and reconstructed by* **Bruce Cochrane**, *Mississauga, Canada.* Photograph by Peter Hogan.

The top and bottom sections are press-moulded and are connected by a squared-off thrown cylinder. The neck and collar are thrown and cut to fit the press-moulded shoulder. The lid is thrown and the handle pulled.

7 *Earthenware teapot, height: 22.5 cm (9 in.) by* **Carol Gouthro**, *Seattle, USA.*

8 *Earthenware teapot, height: 26.5 cm (11 in.) by* **Carol Gouthro**, *Seattle, USA.*
Carol's teapots have slipcast terracotta bodies with handbuilt handles, spouts, etc. They are decorated using a variety of underglazes, glazes and lustres. Her inspiration comes from many sources – botanical forms, ornamentalism, American 1950s vintage fabric, Art Deco and Noritake Ware.

The bodies of Carol's teapots are inspired by a stylised oak leaf. The original models were constructed out of wood and two-part plaster slipcast moulds were made. Using these moulds, Carol casts her teapot bodies in terracotta slip.

Sometimes Carol lays the form down horizontally, and cuts the lid out of the side, and adds feet to the bottom. At other times she stands the form up, creates a base and cuts a lid out of the top. She enjoys making branch-like handles, acorn feet, carving faux-bois, and using other illusionist and trompe l'oeil techniques in her designs.

Colour, pattern and texture are all important elements in her work. Carol uses underglazes to lay down

patterns because she wants the precision they offer. She uses a lot of black-and-white wax resist technique and also sgraffitto through layers of underglaze, to create texture and depth, as well as coloured glazes and lustres to add a jewel-like quality to the pieces. Contrast is an important element in her designs – the contrast between shiny and matt, textured and smooth surfaces.

9 *Sculptural teapot, height: 80 cm (32 in.) by* **Brad Schwieger**, *Ohio, USA.*
The work is wheel-thrown and then altered, mostly by cutting away the clay with a wire tool. Spouts and handles are either thrown or press-moulded. Brad applies glazes and slips before firing in a soda and salt kiln.

10 *Sculptural teapot, height: 75 cm (30 in.) by* **Brad Schwieger**, *Ohio, USA.*

11 *Porcelain teapot with fluted decoration and a cane handle, height: 25 cm (10 in.) by* **David Leach**, *Devon, England.*
David started work in the 1930s with his father, Bernard Leach, at the Leach Pottery, St Ives. He now lives and works at the Lowerdown Pottery in Devon, England, and has been making teapots for over 65 years. This is an example of a porcelain teapot with fluted decoration and cane handle. Fluting can be done with either a metal or wooden tool when the clay is leatherhard. Resting the teapot in his lap for support, the fluting action is achieved in a single

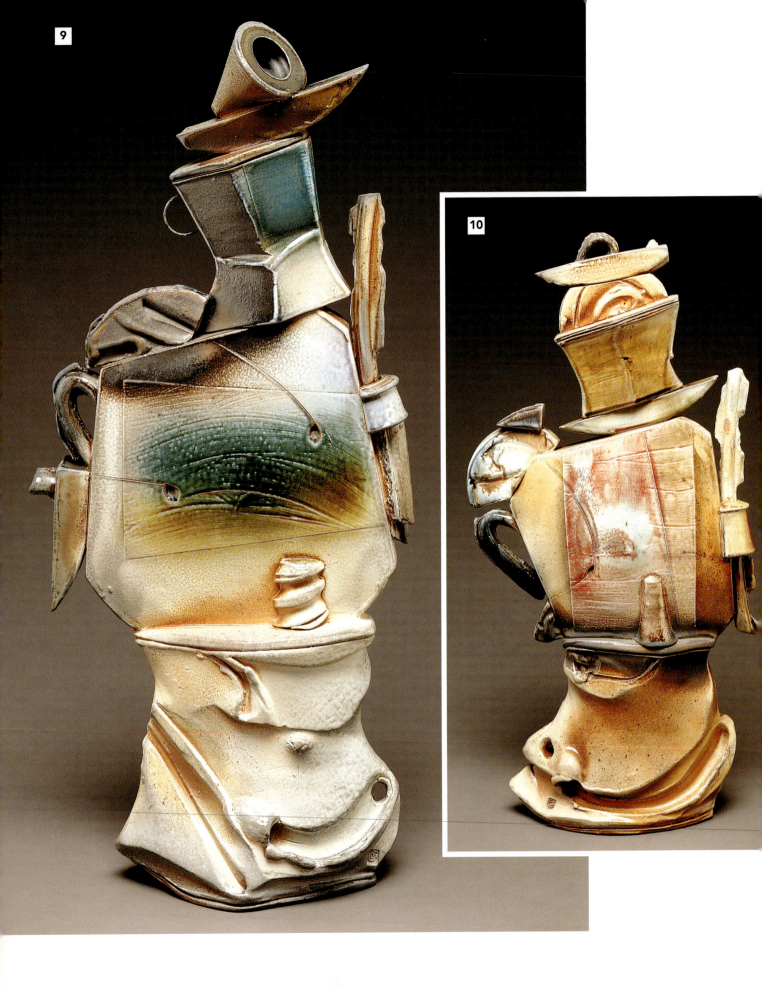

11

dynamic stroke – David says, 'never hesitate, be confident and relaxed'. The aim is to achieve a regular rhythmic fluting which enhances the form of the teapot body.

The teapot is glazed with a Y'Ching glaze and fired to 1280°C (2336°F) in reduction.

12 *Porcelain teapot, height: 20 cm (8 in.) by* **Bridget Drakeford**, *Hereford, England. Copper crackle glaze/rosewood and silver fittings, oxidised firing.* Photograph by Lynda Medwell.

The majority of Bridget's inspiration for her teapots comes from the classical forms of both European and Oriental traditions, where she tries to reflect their simplicity in her own shapes.

All her teapots are thrown on the wheel, biscuit fired and glazed to 1280°C (2336°F). She usually works on four or six teapots at a time, using the same body shape but altering and carving where appropriate.

Bridget mainly uses wood or cane handles as she likes the mixture of materials, with silver or gold as finishing touches. Two good friends help her in this – a wood turner who makes the knobs and handle uprights, and a jeweller who makes the beaten silver handles and the silver tops for the knobs. There is a silver threaded rod which runs through the centre of these pieces and it is held in place with a silver burr. Bridget makes the silver rings used to secure the cane handles. She says that she is always thinking of new ways to add a different dimension to a classical teapot, but never forgetting that they must pour well and not drip!

13 *Porcelain teapot, height: 18 cm (7 in.) by* **Bridget Drakeford**. *Rich black glaze, ebony and silver fittings, reduction firing.* Photograph by Lynda Medwell.

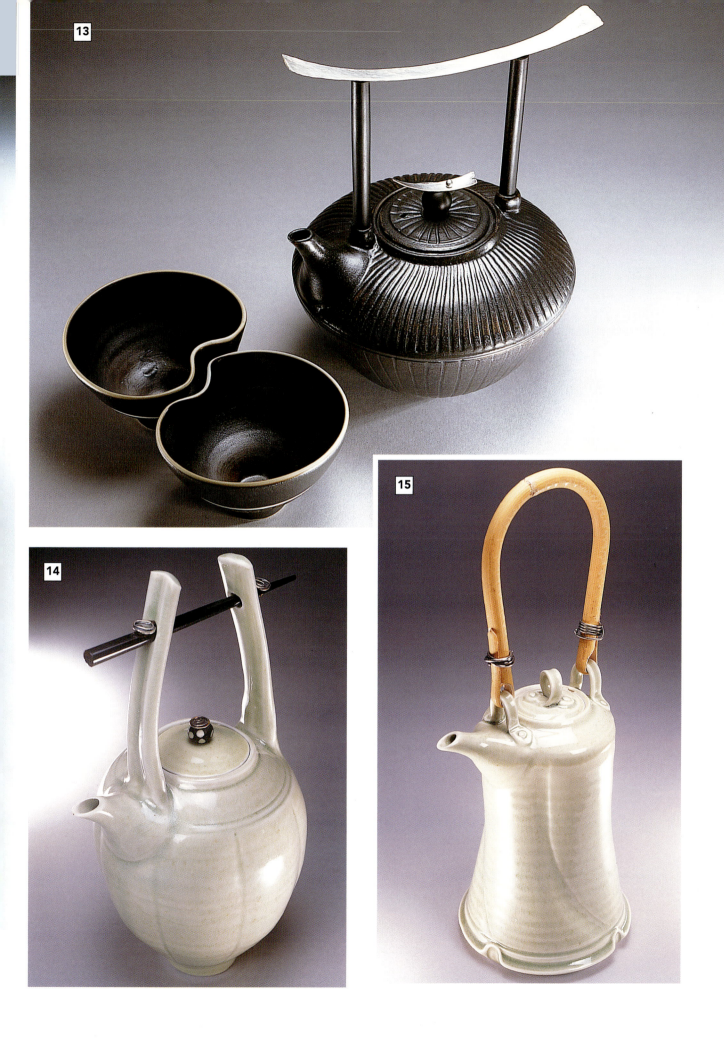

14 *Porcelain teapot, height: 22.5 cm (9 in.) with ebony cross bar held in place by two silver pins, by* **Bridget Drakeford**. Photograph by Lynda Medwell.

15 *Porcelain teapot with cane handle, height: 18 cm (7 in.), by* **Bridget Drakeford**. Photograph by Lynda Medwell.

16 *Wood-fired teapot, height: 25 cm (9.5 in.), by* **Linda Christianson**, *Minnesota, USA.*

Linda's work is made on a treadle wheel using stoneware clay and decorated with a few slips. The wood kiln and its changing atmosphere combined with a bit of salt, produces a dappled, variable surface. She says she wants the pots to function well yet satisfy her aesthetic interest.

17 *Spherical teapot by* **Tavs Jorgensen** *for Dartington Pottery.*

This teapot is constructed from simple geometric elements. It is an uncompromising utilitarian design with aesthetics guided by the function of the object. Its spherical shape is the optimum for retaining heat. The lid is positioned in a tilted back position, which prevents it from falling off during use, and features a knob designed to nest the forefinger when lifting. The wiggled spout ensures a drip-free pour and the small knob on the handle aids a secure grip.

18 *Group of three teapots designed by* **Janice Tchalenko** *in 1983 for Dartington Pottery, Devon, England.*

Originally thrown, the teapots are now slipcast and used as a vehicle for pattern and reactive glazes by different Dartington designers. The three patterns are:

1. 'Quilt' by Petra Tilly – a mixture of matt and shiny glazes applied by sponge, brush and slip trailer.
2. 'Ruskin Blue' by Stephen Course – red and blue reactive glaze.
3. 'Forget-Me-Knot' by Ann Bolin – sponged flowers on a reactive blue glaze.

19 Escaping Frog, *teapot by* **Roger Law** *(adopted from Tavs Jorgensen) for Dartington Pottery.*

This teapot is slipcast with modelled additions. Roger Law used to be famous as the creative energy behind the television show 'Spitting Image', ridiculing the rich and famous. He now resides in Australia and uses Dartington Pottery as a studio base for his ceramic work.

20 *Earthenware teapot, height: 12.5 cm (5 in.), by* **Clive Bowen**, *Devon, England.*

Clive works at the Shebbear Pottery in Devon, where for over 30 years he has been making traditional domestic ware with English slipware decoration. His teapots are thrown using red earthenware (Fremington clay). The top half was dipped in the white slip and a black slip applied to the lower half. A green slip-trailed decoration was then applied using a slip-trailing bulb. Glazed in a transparent glaze and once-fired to cone 03–04 (1060°C– 1100°C/ 1940°F– 2014°F) in a wood-fired kiln, resulting in beautiful variations in colour.

21 *Earthenware teapot, height: 12.5 cm (5 in.) by* **Clive Bowen**, *Devon, England.*

At leatherhard, this thrown teapot was dipped into a white slip. The slip was left for a few seconds and then the decoration combed through using a rubber tool. Glazed in a transparent glaze and once-fired to cone 03–04 (1060°C– 1100°C/ 1940°F–2014°F) in a wood-fired kiln.

22 *Porcelain teapot, height: 10 cm (4 in.), by* **Geoffrey Swindell**, *Cardiff, Wales.*

Geoff has been working on a miniature scale since 1970, making porcelain vessels normally less than 12 cm (5 in.) high. He is inspired by a wide variety of visual sources, including marine life, science-fiction, fossils, tin-plate toys, and objects found on the beaches of South Wales, eroded by sea and time. All the constituent parts of Geoff's teapots, including the handles, are made on the wheel in porcelain and fired to cone 8 (1263°C/2305°F). Geoff's small vessels are often deeply textured and pitted, creating an organic feel. However, this technique distorts the form in firing, due to the stress incurred in the texturing process, and cannot be used on his teapots.

Geoff sprays up to three glazes and a variety of colouring oxides (including copper, rutile, vanadium and manganese) on each piece. On some pots he creates visual and physical textures by using vanadium oxide to interrupt or resist the flow of the glaze as it begins to melt.

23 *Porcelain teapot, height: 10 cm (4 in.), by* **Geoffrey Swindell**, *Cardiff, Wales.*

24 *Porcelain teapot, height: 10 cm (4 in.), by* **Geoffrey Swindell**, *Cardiff, Wales.*

25 *Porcelain Chartreuse 'stretched' teapot, height: 10 cm (4 in.), by* **Fong Choo**, *Kentucky, USA.*
Photograph by Bob Payne.

This teapot is again thrown on the wheel. Once he has a cylinder form, Fong then carves vertical (or diagonal) lines into the body. Continuing to throw out the belly of the pot results in this interesting carved surface.

26 Tangerina, *porcelain teapot, height: 10 cm (4 in.), by* **Fong Choo**, *Kentucky, USA.*
Photograph by Bob Payne.

Fong makes a range of miniature teapots. They are primarily porcelain, wheel-thrown and, after biscuiting, glazed with jewel tone colours. He then uses another glaze ('Dirty Snow') that fires two cones

20

21

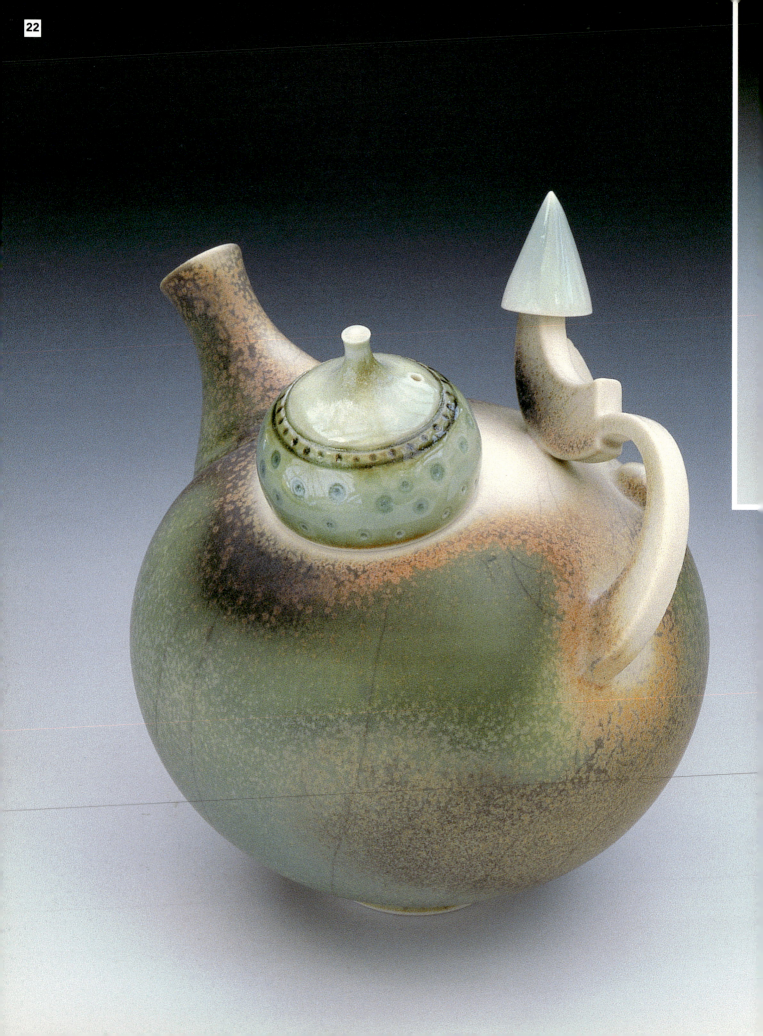

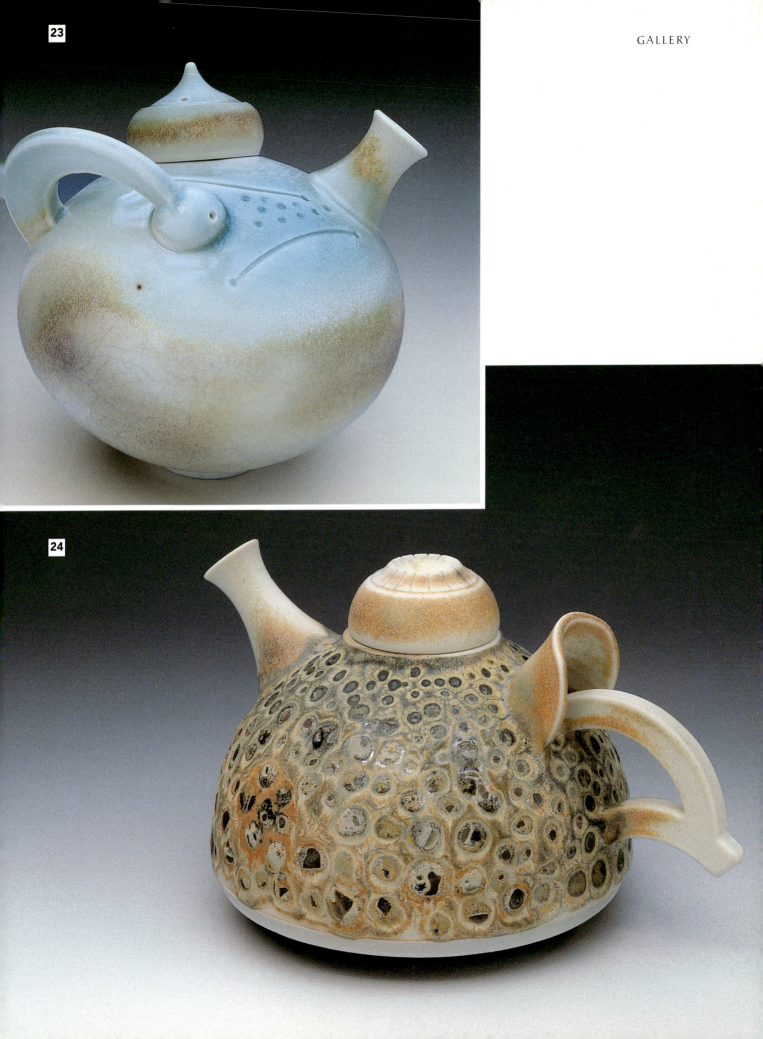

23

24

lower (cone 4/1186°C/2167°F) as an accent on his handles and spouts. Care is required here as it is extremely runny. The pieces are fired in an oxidising atmosphere in an electric kiln to cone 6 (1222°C/2232°F). What is interesting here is that he uses glazes that are suited for cone 04 (1060°C/1940°F) temperatures and then high fires them to cone 6. The accent on the shoulder is layered with Mayco Crystal CG 716, a cone 04 glaze.

The handles are made from soft clay and added when firm. The finished piece is biscuited, glazed, then fired to cone 06 (1000°C/1832°F) in an electric kiln.

27 *Salt-glazed teapot by* **Jane Hamlyn**, *Yorkshire, England.*
The teapot body is thrown without a base and, when leatherhard, an angled section is removed so that the pot slopes backwards. The top section is then joined to a base. The handles are modelled from coils rolled on to a textured surface, flattened on one side, curled into shape and left to stiffen before being joined to the teapot body.

Jane Hamlyn's spouts are made in two sections from thin slabs – the bottom is pressed into a bisque mould and then the top is cut and joined. This method is laborious but at least the spouts don't twist! The teapot is salt glazed to stoneware.

28 *Salt-glazed teapots by* **Jane Hamlyn**, *Yorkshire, England.*

26

29 *Salt-glazed teapot, height: 18 cm (7 in.), by* **Jeremy Nichols***, London, England.*

Jeremy's teapots are constructed from thrown bodies (made in two parts) and lids, with slipcast handles and spouts. These components are joined when leatherhard using Ian Pirie's joining paste (see recipe on p.218).

The moulds for the handles are made by carving a model from a plaster block and taking a mould from it. The moulds for the spouts are made from a thrown solid spout-sized cone which is given a bend when still soft and carved to its final shape when leatherhard. The resulting moulds are two- or four-piece according to the shapes.

After biscuit firing, selected areas are sprayed with a shino glaze (equal parts ball clay, soda feldspar and nepheline syenite) and then with various combinations of blue and black stains to get variations of colour, tone and depth. Glazed areas give a smooth surface, unglazed give the characteristic salt glaze 'orange peel'. During the salt firing to cone 9 (1280°C/2336°F) flat, the handles have to be supported to prevent them from bending and slumping under their own weight during the latter stages of the firing.

30 *Salt-glazed teapot, height: 18 cm (7 in.), by* **Jeremy Nichols***, London, England.*

31 *Handbuilt porcelain teapot, height: 15 cm (6 in.) by* **Karen Orsillo**, *Maine, USA.* Photograph by Robert Diamante.

Karen works with coloured porcelain, which works aesthetically for her as she enjoys the directness of the colour in the clay, making it intrinsic to the form so that she no longer depends on glazes for decoration. She has always enjoyed patternmaking, and working with coloured clay allows her to play with pattern.

Her teapots are constructed from slabs of coloured porcelain. She works with the clay as wet as possible, which challenges her construction skills but avoids some of the technical problems such as cracking of joins. Paramount to this process is allowing the pots to dry slowly.

Ceramic stain colourants are first wedged into the white porcelain. A block of pattern is then built using a variety of colours and colour blends, sometimes using as many as 50 or 60 layers in a block. From this block Karen cuts slabs of clay on the cross-section to reveal the pattern. Using these thin slabs she then constructs her teapots using paper templates and biscuited formers. The handles are often hollow so that the pot can have volume without weight.

She glazes inside the pot and leaves the outside unglazed. The teapot is fired in oxidation to cone 8 (1263°C/2305°F).

32 *Handbuilt porcelain teapot, height: 15 cm (6 in.) by* **Karen Orsillo**, *Maine, USA.* Photograph by Robert Diamante.

33 *Handbuilt porcelain teapot, height: 15 cm (6 in.) by* **Karen Orsillo**, *Maine, USA.* Photograph by Robert Diamante.

34 *Red sandblasted carved stoneware teapot, height: 55 cm (22 in.) by* **Jim Connell**, *South Carolina, USA.*

Jim strives for beauty and elegance in each of his pieces. 'On my very best days in the studio', he says, 'I get a glimpse of it. My art is always about that eternal, elusive quest for beauty.'

This teapot is a large, oversized, decorative teapot. It was thrown using stoneware clay, paddled at the leatherhard (or cheesehard) state, carved and then fired to cone 10 (1305°C/2381°F) in the gas reduction kiln.

Jim uses a unique copper, carbon-trap glaze. It initially comes out of the high-fire kiln with a dull, smoky gunmetal finish. It is then sandblasted which takes off the top, smoky layer, revealing the rich, crackle red surface underneath. The sandblasting process renders the ware non-functional.

35 *Red sandblasted carved stoneware teapot, height: 33 cm (13 in.) by* **Jim Connell**, *South Carolina, USA.*

36 Big Pumpkin Teapot, *height: 50 cm (20 in.) by* **Kate Malone**, *London, England.*

37 Time for Tea, *width: 2m (6½ ft),* by **Kate Malone**, *London, England.*
Time for Tea *is situated in Bentalls Shopping Centre, Kingston-upon-Thames, England. The teapot on top of the clock steams on the hour.*

38 Mother Teapot *by* **Kate Malone**, *London, England.*

39 *Wood-fired stoneware teapot, height: 22.5 cm (9 in.) by* **John Leach**, *Somerset, England.*

40 *Wood-fired stoneware teapot, height: 22.5 cm (9 in.) by* **John Leach**, *Somerset, England.*

41 *Wood-fired stoneware teapot with cane handle, height: 22.5 cm (9 in.) by* **John Leach**, *Somerset, England.*

John creates a range of wheel-thrown kitchen pots based on the strength of English stoneware country pottery. All his pots are wood fired in a three-chambered 350 cu. ft (10 m³) Noborigama (climbing kiln), which holds in the region of 2000 pots. It is fired to cone 12 (1330°C/2426°F) over a 36–37 hour period, which requires John and four other colleagues to take turns in shifts.

The wood used is hazel and Douglas Fir offcuts from a local fencing firm, which sources its timber locally from west Somerset and Devon. John loves the wood-fire finish, but of course it can be rather unpredictable. He sums this up by saying, 'some pots are blessed by

36

37

38

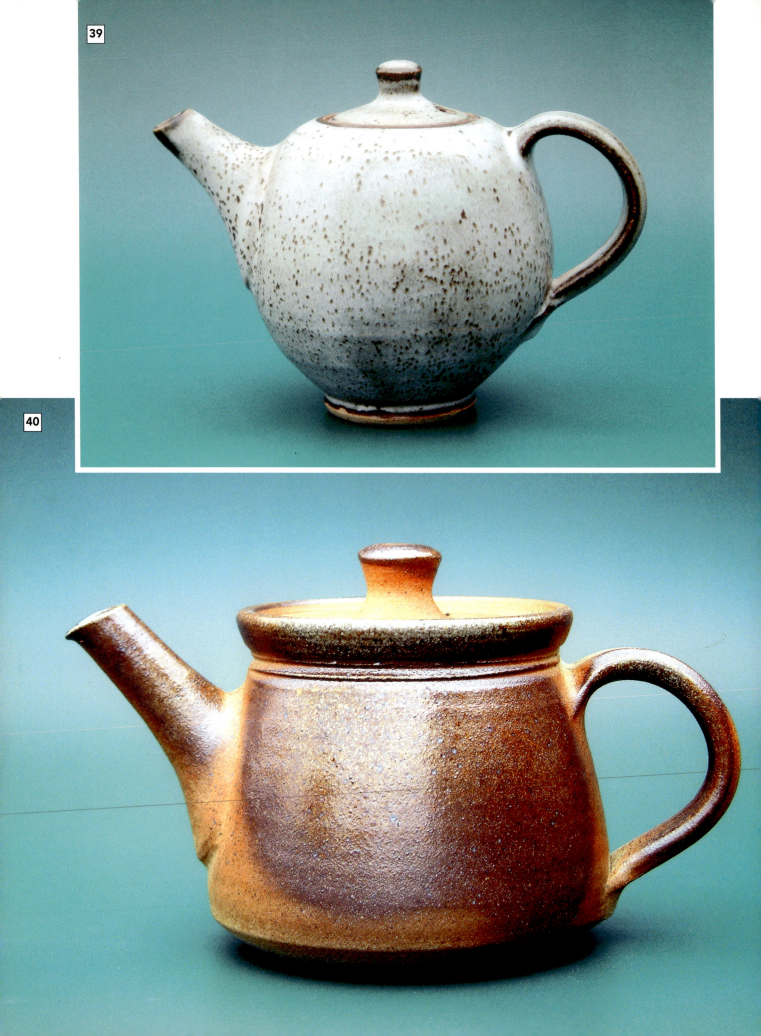

39

40

42

41

fire and some are cursed by fire'. Despite this, he recommends optimism and patience; one of his quotes being, 'Potters of the world ignite!'

42 *Wood-fired stoneware teapot, height: 22.5 cm (9 in.) by* **John Leach**, *Somerset, England.*

43 *Earthenware teapot, height: 12.5 cm (5 in.) by* **John Pollex**, *Plymouth, England.*
John sees his work as three-dimensional paintings where the pots become the canvas.

He throws his teapots with a white earthenware clay and assembles them in the normal way, before dipping them in black slip. When the background slip is almost leatherhard, coloured slips are applied, initially with sponges. This is done to plot out the shapes and marks that John is going to develop.

The colours are obtained using ceramic body stains mixed into a white slip made from the throwing body. As the process continues, John intensifies the colours. This is done by applying more neat body stains to the original colours on the palette. Different tonal effects can be obtained by using different textured sponges, subtly applying one colour onto another, allowing the underneath colour to show through. The dots are applied with a brush; and the final decorative statements are made with a variety of brushes to give a more painterly finish to the work. The pots are biscuit fired to 1050°C (1922°F)

and glaze fired to 1100°C (2012°F).

44 *Earthenware teapot, height: 12.5 cm (5 in.) by* **John Pollex**, *Plymouth, England.*

45 *Soda-glazed teapots by* **Lisa Hammond**, *London, England, with willow handle woven at the end, by Lee Dalby. Height: 22.5 cm (9 in.).*

46 *Soda-glazed teapots by* **Lisa Hammond**, *London, England, with woven willow handle by Lee Dalby, height: 22.5 cm (9 in.)*

47 Black & White, *in earthenware, by* **Mark Dally**, *Staffordshire, England.*
Mark makes his 'Black & White' ware as a bold, contemporary take on traditional Staffordshire slipware. Other design influences include 1950s surface pattern such as Ridgeway's 'Homemaker', and the motifs and calligraphic styles of pre-Hispanic Mexican and Australian aboriginal art.

The teapot is slipcast in high-fired white earthenware and decorated using traditional slip trailing and brushed slip techniques. It is finished in a third firing with platinum lustre applied to the handles and knobs.

48 *Oval teapot, height: 12.5 cm (5 in.) in feathered copper green, by* **Kevin de Choisy**, *Glastonbury, England.*
Kevin is fascinated by the versatility of the polychrome and Creamware glazes that were

developed in England during the Industrial Revolution by Thomas Whieldon, William Greatbatch and their contemporaries.

The body and lid were both thrown. When the pot is leather-hard, Kevin cuts a parallel slice through the centre, leaving two chords of a circle. These are then scored, slipped and luted together. The pot is then dried very slowly to avoid warping. When the clay begins to turn in colour, the slipcast spout and handle are added. Although this goes against common practice, Kevin found that you could join cast and throwing bodies if you waited for the thrown body to become quite dry (i.e., do most of its shrinking). However, he has to admit that he has had so much trouble with the body warping using the above method that he now casts this as well!

To decorate, Kevin first trails the iron-bearing, yellow/orange glaze which he then masks out by painting latex over it. The whole pot is then sprayed with four coats of a blue/turquoise base. A copper-bearing glaze is trailed over the entire pot and the latex is then removed from the iron spots. Finally, Kevin sponges minute areas with a combination of oxides that bleed during the firing.

48

49 *Shino teapot, height: 25 cm (10 in.) by* **Malcolm Davis**, *West Virginia, USA.* Photograph by James Dee.

Malcolm's studio is on top of a mountain in West Virginia, USA, where he works exclusively in porcelain. For him, the joy and the challenge comes from making things that will become an intimate part of the daily lives of others – pots that will be held, eaten from, poured from and sipped from. For Malcolm, making pots is a way to celebrate the mundane rituals of daily life.

The style of Malcolm's work and the nature of the forms are simple and fluid. In searching for glazes that would not compete with the form, but allow the pot to assert its own life and liveliness, he began experimenting with shino glazes, and developed a red shino that provided a lively surface for his work but did not distract from the subtleties of the forms.

Malcolm's work is inspired by Japanese folk traditions. Whether we observe the early pots of the 1st century in Korea, or the dung-fired pots of the original inhabitants of the Americas, they were all made to be used. These pots were often primitive and fragile, but always embodied a feeling of warmth and friendliness from their pure functional intent and the simple processes of their making.

All Malcolm's teapots are formed on the wheel and assembled. They are fired to cone 10 (1305°C/2381°F) in a reduction kiln, with an hour's heavy, smoky reduction early in the firing between cones 012 and 010 (884°C and 900°C/1623°F and 1652°F).

50 *Detail of shino teapot, height: 15 cm (6 in.) by* **Malcolm Davis**, *West Virginia, USA.* Photograph by James Dee.

51 *Shino teapot, height: 22.5 cm (9 in.) by* **Malcolm Davis**, *West Virginia, USA.* Photograph by James Dee.

52 Leopard Print Carwash Skirt, *height: 83 cm (33 in.) by* **Lisa Krigel**, *Cardiff, Wales.*

Lisa says that her teapots are an attempt to blur the boundaries of form and function. They are based on the female form and raise issues of the voyeur's understanding of object, where blatantly adorned figures with attitude appear hermaphroditic with the placing of a functional spout.

Recently her work has veered towards the sculptural, with many teapots almost 1 m (3 ft) in height, using a synthesis of imagery taken from the history of female fashion and fetishism. These influences are as diverse as Victorian corsetry, highstreet fashion and haute couture.

Each teapot is constructed using a combination of slab, coil and pinch techniques. They are then painted using underglazes and fired to 1140°C (2084°F). A transparent glaze is sprayed over the piece and fired to 1100°C (2012°F). Ceramic transfers (fired to 820°C/1508°F)

and/or lustres (fired to 740°C/ 1364°F) are then added. A variety of feathers, beads and rhinestones finish off each teapot.

53 Blue and Silver Mini-Dress, *height: 84 cm (33 in.) by* **Lisa Krigel**, *Cardiff, Wales.*

54–6 Gaia's Nightwatch Sleepytime, *teapot, height: 43 cm (17 in.) by* **Marko Fields**, *Minnesota, USA.*

Marko is enamoured with vessels, not so much because of their functionality, but metaphorically, as they contain liquid, nurture, pour and serve – significant activities amongst humans. Stylistically, his work is often animated and anthropomorphic, usually decorated with pattern fields that have emerged as his signature.

He employs many techniques: slab- and handbuilding, throwing and altering. He also likes to combine different clay bodies within a piece, for the sake of visual contrast and because his ceramic professor told him he couldn't!

Marko's intricately raised and textured surfaces are often achieved using a technique he developed during his graduate studies, which he refers to as 'printmaking in clay'. After pouring a large plaster slabmould, he may spend up to a month carving directly into the plaster, creating a press-mould from which he can pull large clay slabs to build parts of his forms.

After biscuiting, Marko usually covers the pot completely with an

underglaze (Amaco velour black), then wipes off the highlights with a sponge. The teapots are fired to cone 6 (1222°C/ 2232°F) with a subsequent lustre firing.

57 *Ash-glazed teapot, height: 22.5 cm (9 in.), by* **Mike Dodd**, *Somerset, England.*

Mike creates his pots utilising the rocks, clays, wood ashes and silts around him. He is very much of the Leach and Cardew tradition. His work portrays a strength and dignity, revealing the softness of clay from which it is formed.

Here the teapot body has been faceted, providing a frame for a simple combed decoration. The teapot is glazed in a granite-based ash glaze with added iron oxide and fired to 1300°C (2372°F) in a reduction kiln.

58 *Ash-glazed teapot, height: 22.5 cm (9 in.), by* **Mike Dodd**, *Somerset, England.*

59 *Porcelain teapot, height: 22.5 cm (9 in.) by* **Mel Jacobson**, *Minnesota, USA.*

Mel is a Japanese trained functional potter who insists that his teapots work as intended, to make and serve tea. The spout is the key to this, and is cut with a razor knife so that it does not drip.

This teapot is made from domestic porcelain with 25% stoneware added. Additional Lake Superior iron sand is added to create speckles – some call this 'dirty porcelain'. The glaze is a

55

56

Sung style, clear/semi-matt with Mel's orange glaze, fired to cone 11 (1315°C/2399°F) just bending. See p.217 for glaze recipes.

60 *Porcelain teapots, height: 30 cm (12 in.) by* **Meira Mathison**, *British Columbia, Canada.*
Photograph by Janet Dwyer.

The teapot body is thrown without a bottom, altered, and then a slab is added as a base. A similar slab is added at the top. Coloured clay additions (using encapsulated stains to keep the orange/yellow/red colours) and stamped images of leaves are applied to the teapot body.

Meira makes these teapots in pairs, in such a way that they nestle together. One side of the taller teapot is altered to be a kind of a kidney shape, into which the smaller teapot can snuggle.

The bottom of the teapots are designed with a rim to catch the melting and flowing glazes. After biscuiting, the teapots are glazed inside using Meira's black/brown glaze *(see p.216)*. Glazes are layered, starting at the foot with a glaze that is very stable to allow other glazes to melt down into it without the glaze flowing off the pot. Next, a light layer of matt blue glaze is applied, before the upper area is sprayed with spotted black, and a light over-spray with copper-blue.

Lastly, a dusting of powdered wood ash on the upper area creates the glaze-runs that characterise Meira's work. A note of warning here: this combination of glazes is very volatile and you must protect

60

61

your kiln shelves accordingly. The pots are reduction fired to cone 10 (1305°C/2381°F) in a gas kiln.

61 *Porcelain teapot with accessories, height: 30 cm (12 in.)* by **Meira Mathison**, *British Columbia, Canada.* Photograph by Janet Dwyer.

62 *Teapots, height: (various) approx. 15 cm (6 in.)* by **Peter Beard**, *Warwickshire, England.*
Peter makes one-off ceramics that are modern but also owe an allegiance to historic works from a variety of sources – landscapes, modern and ancient Egyptian culture, and the shape and form of the desert sands sculpted by the winds.

Peter does not make domestic ware and his teapots are non-functional; he describes them as 'humorous teapots'. They have been specially created for themed exhibitions in which he has been invited to participate.

Peter makes two types of teapots. The round teapot is made from a pinched body, the lid being an integral part of this non-functional piece. An airhole is made in the base of the pot to allow the air to escape during firing. The handle and spout, which are both solid, are made by rolling and pinching. The flat teapots are made by rolling out the body from a piece of clay. All the teapot elements are assembled onto the leatherhard body from soft clay. An additional leg is attached at the back of the flat sectioned

teapot to allow it to be stable on three points.

After biscuiting, the teapots are decorated in accordance with his other themed work. Peter uses water-based wax resist decoration with layers of different glazes. These glazes have a variety of different maturing temperatures, which, when fired to 1280°C (2336°F) result in a range of textures from matt to satin matt. Peter uses a whole variety of stains and oxides to achieve the specific colour he requires.

63 *Teapot, height: 15 cm (6 in.)* by **Peter Beard**, *Warwickshire, England.*

64 *Teapot, height: 12.5 cm (5 in.)* by **Peter Beard**, *Warwickshire, England.*

65 *Salt-glazed teapot, height: 12.5 cm (5 in.),* by **Phil Rogers**, *Rhyader, Wales.*
Phil Rogers makes a range of ash- and salt-glazed work. The beauty of Phil's pots comes from his direct approach to the clay. Here the teapot body is impressed with rope and then a grass motif inscribed using a sharp tool. After a biscuit firing the teapot is glazed with his standard ash glaze (*see recipe on p.217*), before being salt fired to cone 11 (1315°C/2399°F). The fluxing effects of the sodium vapour have increased the fluidity of the glaze, resulting in a more textured surface than one would expect from the same glaze in a normal reduction firing.

66 *Salt-glazed teapot, 12.5 cm (5 in.),* by **Phil Rogers**, *Rhyader, Wales.*
This teapot has been dipped in an orange slip, then salt glazed to cone 11.

67 *Stoneware teapot, height: 20 cm (8 in.),* by **Jeff Oestreich**, *Minnesota, USA.*
Jeff throws his teapots on the wheel and then alters them, though on initial viewing they look slab-built. Jeff is often questioned on this point and his response is that there are subtle references to wheel work that are very important to him. He likes to explore the polarities of soft and hard edge, full and lean volume, matt and shiny surface. Additionally, the glazes are selected to highlight these interests.

68 *Porcelain teapot with copper handle, height: 25 cm (10 in.),* by **Tom Turner**, *Ohio, USA.*
Tom works with Gail Russell at their Peachblow Pottery. The teapot is thrown in porcelain and the sides are then faceted using a potato peeler. The pot is glazed after biscuiting, with a glaze that is simply made from a clay that lies beneath Tom's house; all he does is ballmill it. The piece is fired in a reduction kiln to cone 9 (1280°C/2336°F), creating these beautiful tea-dust crystals, and hare's-fur streaks.

The solid copper handle is made by Tom from electrical cable and plumbers' caps which are soldered, oxidised, and polished.

62

63

64

191

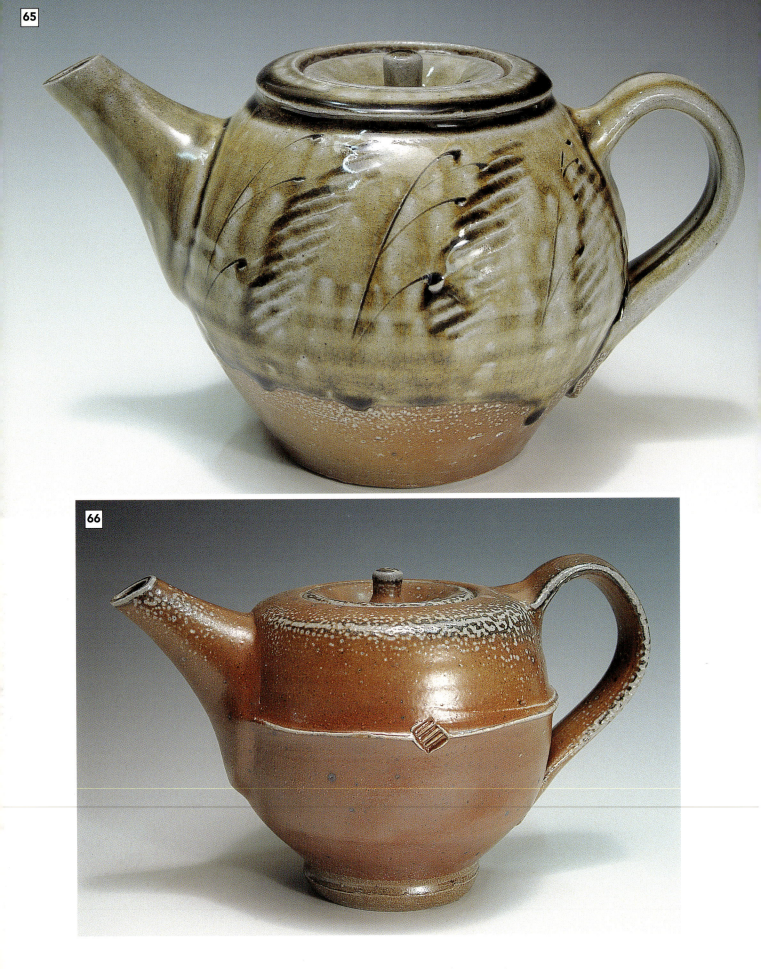

67

68

69 *Handbuilt stoneware teapot, height: 60 cm (24 in.), by* **Nolan Babin**, *California, USA.* Photograph by Cathy Murphy.

Nolan's teapot is built from slabs that are made from wheel-thrown parts, allowed to stiffen to leather-hard, scored, slipped and then assembled. After the teapot is constructed, the top where the lid fits is thrown and developed in the conventional manner. The completed teapot is wood fired to cone 10 (1305°C/2381°F) over a period of four days; this process is vital for the surface to develop.

Nolan does not glaze his teapots as he wants to know what the wood will do to the clay. The texture is enhanced by the flashing of wood ash during the firing, as opposed to covering the surface with glaze. Occasionally he throws in a handful of salt, or sticks of wood soaked in copper and manganese carbonate to give extra colour. This end result is a beautifully warm, wood-fired surface with a somewhat matt finish.

70 *Wood-fired handbuilt teapot, height: 25 cm (10 in.) by* **Randy Johnston**, *Wisconsin, USA.* Photograph by Peter Lee.

71 *Wood-fired handbuilt teapot, height: 22.5 cm (9 in.), by* **Randy Johnston**, *Wisconsin, USA.* Photograph by Peter Lee.

Randy's teapots are made using paper and wood patterns for the spouts, handles and parts of the body. They are cut, assembled and altered as needed.

Randy works with ideas of function, but he is always considering the sculptural intent. All pieces are decorated with a kaolin slip and are wood fired. Randy focuses on surface texture, carefully controlling the periods of reduction to enhance the reds.

72 *Earthenware teapot, height: 22.5 cm (9 in.) by* **Peter Dick**, *Yorkshire, England.*
Peter electric fires to 1080°C (1976°F) which gives him the possibility of using brightly coloured slips, such as copper green, to decorate the earthenware. His aim is to produce pots that do their job perfectly – feel comfortable in the hand and on the lip, and pour well, etc. but also give amusement and pleasure.

The modelled knobs and handles, inspired by the folk ceramics of central Europe and Mexico, are fun to make and seem to produce a smile; 'enjoyment', says Peter, 'is a two way thing'. The glazes are regularly tested for safety and Peter is careful to avoid the use of copper in contact with food.

73 *Wood-fired stoneware teapots, height: 22.5 cm (10 in.), by* **Winchcombe Pottery**. Photograph by John Wheeldon.

74 *Stoneware teapot, height: 25 cm (10 in.), by* **Ray Finch**, *Winchcombe Pottery, Devon, England. Dolomite-glazed, with traditional cane handle, made in the 1980s.*

75 *Salt-glazed teapot, height: 22.5 cm (9 in.) by* **Ray Finch,** *Winchcombe Pottery, Devon, England.* Photograph by John Wheeldon.
Ray Finch took over Winchcombe Pottery from Michael Cardew in 1946, and it ranks alongside St Ives with Bernard Leach as one of the primary pioneering studio potteries in England.

Initially making a range of domestic earthenware, Winchcombe Pottery moved to making stoneware in 1964. Ray handed over the pottery to his son Michael in 1979 but continues to make individual pieces. This is a fine example of one of Ray's salt-glazed teapots.

76 Fireplum Teapot, *height: 37.5 cm (15 in.), by* **Ricky Maldonado,** *California, USA.*

77 Vertigo Teapot, *height: 35 cm (14 in.), by* **Ricky Maldonado,** *California, USA.*

78 Way Out Teapot, *height: 20 cm (8 in.), by* **Ricky Maldonado,** *California, USA.*
His teapots are coil-built from terracotta clay and then layered with six coats of terra sigillata. The teapot is then burnished, initially by hand and then again with soft plastic, resulting in a very tight smooth surface.

At this point Ricky applies the line design with black slip that he makes from the terra sigillata, coloured with a black oxide. He then applies the glaze one dot at

a time using a sable brush. The piece is once-fired at cone 06 (1000°C/1832°F).

79 *Soda-glazed loop handle teapot, height: 22 cm (9 in.), by* **Ruthanne Tudball**, *Norfolk, England.*
Ruthanne makes a wide range of soda pieces that are influenced by natural earth rhythms, including tide patterns. Her work exhibits a softness and fluidity brought about by the direct approach to the clay, resulting in very tactile pieces.

Her teapots are made on the wheel using a light, high silica body that is very plastic for throwing and manipulating. The lid and spout are initially thrown off the hump. The body is then thrown with a thick rounded gallery. Ruthanne often uses a small bamboo harp to cut the facets while the wheel is slowly turning. The rounded facets are basically formed by stretching the clay between the bamboo pieces. Placing one inside, and the other outside, they are used together to draw up and stretch the sides of the body, creating the round faceting. On this particular teapot, the facets were also impressed with a sea shell.

While the teapot body is still on the wheel, Ruthanne alters the gallery for the locking lid (this is shown in detail on p.34). The spout and handle are then added. Other than the feet, the teapot is finished whilst still on the wheel, as wet soft clay. This is a very direct approach,

73

74

75

76

78

199

which is further enhanced by the soda firing. The spout is interesting; it is initially thrown in a trumpet shape and then added immediately to the wet teapot body. When the pot is leatherhard she places three feet on the base to add elegance and buoyancy, allowing light to pass under the form and lift it visually.

The teapot is glazed inside and raw fired in a soda kiln to cone 10 (1305°C/2381°F).

80 *Soda-glazed loop handle teapot, height: 22 cm (9 in.), by* **Ruthanne Tudball**, *Norfolk, England.*

The facets on this teapot were cut with a bamboo harp while the pot was turning on the wheel.

81 *Wood-fired stoneware, by* **Svend Bayer**, *Devon, England.*

Svend throws the teapot body, lid and spout 'off the hump', using a string to cut the pieces off in the Oriental style. As the pieces stiffen, the spout is attached first, then three small feet, and as soon as the feet are able to take the weight, the pulled handle is attached.

The teapot is glazed inside with a celadon glaze and fired in a wood-fired kiln. The pots are stacked as close as possible to each other and rest on wads of fireclay. Svend's firing lasts five days, four of which are above 1280°C (2336°F). The final firing temperature is 1340°C (2444°F).

This particular teapot has been heavily ashed during the firing – larch ash on the side facing the

79

firebox and ash tree ash on the side facing the nearest side-stocking hole. This ash is deposited naturally and not applied. The pot is rapidly cooled in a reduction atmosphere to 900°C (1652°F) and then oxidised.

82 *Soda-fired teapot, height: 22.5 cm (9 in.), by* **Trevor Chaplin**, *Wiltshire, England.*

Trevor throws his teapot using a clay wedged with plenty of silica and Molochite. The biscuit pot was dipped in blue slip, and rutile was brushed over the surface. It was soda glazed in a gas-fired downdraught kiln to a maximum 1330°C (2426°F) – cone 10 flat. Then it was positioned in the kiln very close to the firebox, where it would be most vulnerable to the extreme effects of heat and vapour.

Trevor has a 30 cu. ft (0.9 m³) soda kiln and uses 3 lb (1.3 kg) of sodium bicarbonate per firing. The sodium bicarbonate is diluted in boiling water and sprayed into the kiln when it is over 1200°C (2192°F). This takes between 2 to 3 hours. The kiln soaks for an hour, then is allowed to crash cool to 1000°C (1832°F) before bunging up and leaving it to cool for two days.

83 *Reduced stoneware, 'square-faceted' teapot, height: 20 cm (8 in.) by* **Sequoia Miller**, *Washington, USA.*

Sequoia feels that pottery is kinetic, in that we understand it through action and use – lifting, washing, serving and pouring. This is especially true of teapots, as they

82

suggest movement even when still. Sequoia initially throws the square-faceted teapot as a thick, open bowl form. He then squeezes it square immediately after throwing it. When leatherhard, it is paddled using a small wooden batt to define the planes and corners, then faceted with a long flexible knife.

Inverting the teapot body and re-centring it on the wheel, Sequoia trims out the underside. Removing it from the wheel he cuts out the arcs between the feet using a fettling knife. He then re-centres the pot on the wheel, right side up, and attaches the four feet with little lugs. A coil of clay is attached to the rim of the open square form and thrown to create the lid seat. This can be a little tricky, as the base is square and the lid seat is round. Lastly, Sequoia throws the lid and spout, finishes and attaches them at the leatherhard stage, and puts on handle lugs.

After biscuiting, the pot is glazed with a tenmoku glaze and a rich iron/rutile slip is brushed on. The pot is fired in a gas reduction kiln to cone 10 (1305°C/2381°F).

84 Thalassic Teapot, *reduced stoneware, height: 15 cm (6 in.)* by **Sequoia Miller**, *Washington USA.*
The Thalassic teapot starts with a thrown ring that has no bottom. At soft leatherhard, Sequoia squeezes it flat. When the clay is firm, he shapes the bottom and top profiles of the altered ring using a knife or wood rasp. Sequoia then adds slabs

to enclose the ring with a bottom and top. The spout is a shaped and attached slab. The lid is simply cut out of the top, with an added knob. The handle is pulled, attached wet, and faceted wet. The pot is fired in a gas reduction kiln to cone 10 (1305°C/2381°F).

85 Wyoming Tripod, *wood-fired stoneware, height: 20 cm (8 in.),* by **Steve Hansen**, *Minnesota, USA.* Photograph by Davis Sherwin. The inspiration for Steve's work comes from growing up in the rural mid-West, where his family were involved with carpentry, mechanics and farming. He was particularly influenced by his grandfather's farm, where there were barns full of old tractors, horse harnesses, rusted licence plates, radiator cans and hubcaps. Steve believes that by sharing with others the things that have made us who we are, our understanding of what it means to be human is enhanced.

Steve's teapots are completely handbuilt. He primarily uses slabs for the body, top and bottom of the pot, with handbuilt sticks or other shapes for the handles. The spouts are frequently made using a slab rolled over a wooden dowel, then rolled over an old air conditioner cover to achieve the appearance of a flexible conduit. The licence plate look is achieved by dusting a slab of clay with dry ball clay or kaolin, then pressing it into the back of an actual licence plate. Steve also has simple biscuited press-moulds that he uses for bolt heads.

The colours are applied at the bone-dry stage. Steve uses slips made from a cone 6 (1222°C/2232°F) porcelain, coloured with mason stains, commercial terra sigillata, and oxide washes. The pots are then fired in a cross-draught wood kiln to achieve the slightly random look of natural ageing.

86 Michigan '24 Tea', *wood-fired stoneware, height: 25 cm (10 in.),* by **Steve Hansen**, *Minnesota, USA.* Photograph by Davis Sherwin.

87 Tower Teapot, *height: 42.5 cm (19 in.), by* **Steven McGovney** *and* **Tammy Camarot**, *Arizona, USA.*

88 ½ Round Teapot, *height: 32.5 cm (13 in.), by* **Steven McGovney** *and* **Tammy Camarot**, *Arizona, USA.*
Steven sculpts each piece, and then makes rubber masters to pull plaster-working moulds from. This is especially useful with intricate shapes. The rubber provides easy release from the plaster whereas a solid master may not. Steven and Tammy do not make block- and case-masters, as their output is too small.

Handles are extruded and hand pulled, allowed to dry to shape, and then attached. The pieces are then fired to cone 03 (1100°C/2012°F). Tammy then paints in a water-colour style with commercial underglazes, and uses multicoated application for intense colour. She uses sgraffito decoration for extra detail, painting a layer of white first,

85

86

then a darker colour to scribe through. It makes the lines very clean, and is much easier than actually going in to the fired clay. The pieces are then bisque fired to cone 08 (955°C/1751°F) to set the underglaze, then dipped into clear gloss and fired to cone 05 (1046°C/1915°F). The extra firing enables handling of the fragile forms, and keeps the sgraffito clean.

89 Tango Teapot, *height: 30 cm (12 in.),* by **Steven McGovney** and **Tammy Camarot**, *Arizona, USA.*

90 Submarine Teapot, *height: 18 cm (7 in.),* by **Terry Bell-Hughes**, *Wales. Raw ash over tenmoku.*

91 Elephant Teapot, *height: 22.5 cm (9 in.),* by **Terry Bell-Hughes**, *Wales. Ash glazed.*
Terry was a student on the Harrow Studio Pottery course in the 1970s under Mick Casson and Victor Margrie. He now makes a range of functional pots which have a strong decorative element. The main influences on his work are the Leach tradition and his own dry sense of humour. His elephant decoration he sees as a homage to the potter Denise Wren who made wonderful ceramic elephants.

The teapot body is thrown on the wheel and altered when soft. A thin slab of clay is then rolled out and, in the case of the *Elephant Teapot*, the elephant motif is cut out and the detail inscribed into it. The freshly

87

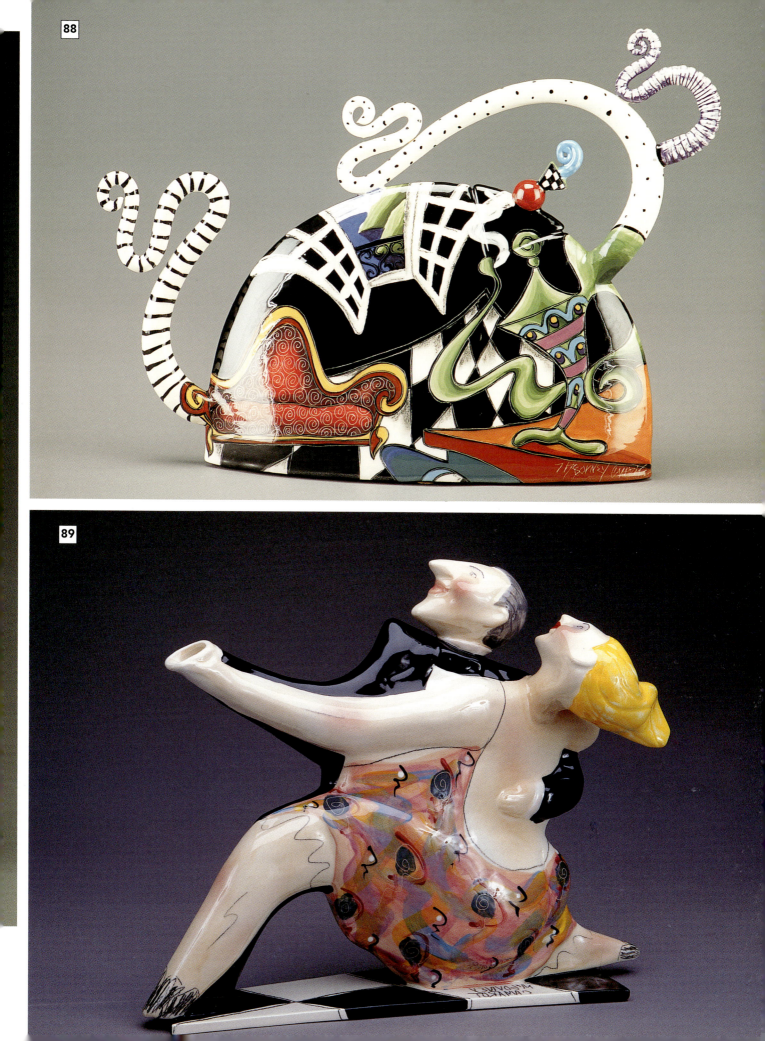

90

91

thrown body is placed on a banding wheel at shoulder height. With the thin elephant slab in one hand, Terry slaps it onto the teapot in one dramatic movement. As Terry says, 'Where it lands is where it stays' – any bits that miss are pushed in or cut away. The spout is thrown and attached wet.

Terry basically has two glazes in his workshop: matt ash and a fluid ash. After biscuiting, Terry applies by brush a variety of coloured glazes to create the coloured areas he desires. He then finally dips the entire pot into the runny ash glaze and it is fired in a reduction kiln to 1300°C (2372°F). Sometimes Terry glazes the entire foot of the teapot and fires it on sea shells in the kiln (the shells prevent the pot sticking to the kiln shelf).

92 *Salt-glazed teapot, height: 20 cm (8 in.), by* **Toff Milway**, *Gloucestershire, England.*

93 *Salt-glazed teapot, height: 22.5 cm (9 in.), by* **Toff Milway**, *Gloucestershire, England.*
Toff makes a range of once-fired, salt-glazed stoneware. He says that his conventional teapots follow in the Cardew and Finch tradition and he would like them to be in daily use.

When the teapot is leatherhard it is raw glazed and slipped, using the jug and turntable method. Sometimes this method can overwet the surface; when this happens Toff judiciously applies a blowlamp. The salt firing to 1320°C (2408°F)

produces a remarkable range of finely textured surfaces and subtle lustres.

94 *Stoneware teapot, height: 23 cm (9 in.), by* **Will Levi Marshall**, *Dumfries, Scotland.*

95 *Stoneware teapot, height: 23 cm (9 in.), by* **Will Levi Marshall**, *Dumfries, Scotland.*
Will admires nearly all the pots made more than 500 years ago, although he has a special affinity for all ancient Chinese pottery (Tang and Han dynasties in particular), and medieval British pottery.

This example is based on Will's interpretation of the Wedgwood 'Crabstock' teapots – hence it has a grainy texture on the spout and handle. The body and lid are thrown, and the body is altered on the wheel straight after throwing. Both handles are coiled. The spout is formed from a textured slab, which avoids all the issues regarding twisting of thrown spouts. Will also makes sure the spout is attached low on the teapot body to help create good water pressure. As a last touch, he removes any glaze from the edge of the lip to help break the surface tension.

At present, Will prefers the overhead handle, as it mirrors the body beneath, makes the pot easy to lift, and seems to give a visual compactness. However, it is perhaps less popular because cleaning, filling and draining the teapot is more difficult. There is always a delicate balance between aesthetics and function. The teapots are oxidation

fired to cone 9/10 (1280–1305°C/2336°F–2381°F).

96 Feather Teapot, *height: 27 cm (10.5 in.), by* **Virginia Graham**, *Cardiff, Wales. Stoneware.*
Virginia uses a combination of slipcasting and handbuilding techniques to create forms comprised of many components, often placing them out of context. Her surfaces make reference to utilitarian wares from industrial ceramic history, including mochaware, Cornishware and blue & white porcelain.

She mixes a variety of decorative techniques together on each piece, including slip resist, floral onglaze transfers and metallic lustres. This dictates that the teapot can often be fired four times: biscuit to 1060°C (1940°F), glaze fired at 1160°C (2120°F), enamel fired to 860°C (1580°F) and lustre fired to 740°C (1364°F).

97 *Side-handle teapot, height: 10 cm (4 in.), by* **Will Ruggles & Douglass Rankin**, *North Carolina, USA.*
Thrown on the wheel, Will's and Douglass's teapots are fired to cone 9 (1280°C/2336°F) in a neutral atmosphere with wood, salt and soda. They are made with a coarse stoneware, about one third of which is 'wild' clays, which add an indescribable richness.

98 *Porcelain teapot, height: 21 cm (8 in.), by* **West Marshall**, *Buckinghamshire, England.*
Photograph by Stephen Brayne.

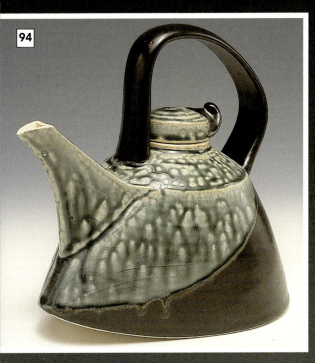

94

95

West is fascinated by the undulating edges and inlaid lines which interact with simple forms. He takes considerable time designing his pieces, although he is careful that they are not 'too designed'.

The teapot body is thrown to create a crisp and clean form. He uses the Southern Ice porcelain from Australia because he says it has a stunning whiteness and beautiful translucent quality. His handles are handbuilt using a variety of techniques, including press-moulding and extruding.

99 *Porcelain teapot, height: 16 cm (6 in.) by* **West Marshall**, *Buckinghamshire, England.* Photograph by Stephen Brayne.

98

99

Conclusion

I HOPE I HAVE conveyed at least some of my passion for, and commitment to, teapots and given an insight into their broad diversity. The full spectrum of teapots being made today was only really brought home to me during the compiling of this book.

Here are some of the main points that we have explored:

- The slumped-slabbing technique illustrated by Richard Godfrey opens up a whole new world to making shaped vessels.
- Steve Harrison shows that throwing inside a plaster mould is a very exciting and interesting technique with vast potential. This concept could be further explored.
- We have seen how slab-building, cutting and folding the clay into teapot shapes not easily achieved on the wheel, can offer a method of making to handbuilding potters.
- By creating plaster moulds we can again create forms that are unique to this process.
- The core of the book has focused on domestic teapots, which are virtually all thrown on the wheel and conform to the classic construction methods discussed in Chapter Three. Even with these common parameters, we can see a vast diversity and depth of individuality.
- We have analysed a whole series of exciting and innovative handles from potters such as Lisa Hammond, Joanna Howells, Steve Woodhead, Bridget Drakeford, Tom Turner and Jeremy Nichols.
- There is a variety of exciting and innovative spouts from potters such as Ruthanne Tudball, Peter Meanley, Walter Keeler, and many others.
- Morgen Hall, Chris Myers, Ricky Maldonado, Peter Ilsley, Malcolm Davis, and many others, have shared their superb decorative techniques.

Where now? Well, I'm back in my workshop with a hundred new ideas to explore. I hope you will be eager to get back to your workshop feeling suitably inspired.

And for all of you who collect these wonderful teapots, I hope I have given you a greater understanding of our world, and shown the love, passion and commitment we have for our subject.

I've run out of time and space so I will end by saying, 'Lets put the kettle on and have a cup of tea. . .

Now, which teapot shall I use?'

List of Suppliers

UK Suppliers

Bath Potters Supplies
Unit 18, Fourth Avenue,
Westfield Trading Estate,
Radstock, BA3 4XE
Tel: 01761 411077
Fax: 01761 414115
www.bathpotters.co.uk

Briar Wheels and Suppliers Ltd
Whitsbury Road, Fordingbridge,
Hants, SP6 1NQ
Tel: 01425 652991
Fax: 01425 656188
www.briarwheels.co.uk

Brick House Ceramic Supplies
The Barn, Sheepcotes Lane,
Silver End, Witham,
Essex, CM8 3PJ
Tel: 01376 585655
Fax: 01376 585656
Email: enquiries@brickhouse
ceramics.co.uk
www.brickhouseceramics.co.uk

Ceramatech Ltd
Units 16 & 17, Frontier Works,
Queen Street, London,
N17 8JA
Tel: 020 8885 4492
Fax: 020 365 1363
Email:
ceramatech@potterycrafts.co.uk

Clayman
Morrells Barn, Park Lane,
Lagness, Chichester,
West Sussex, PO20 1LR
Tel: 01243 265845
Fax: 01243 267582
Email: info@the-clayman.co.uk
www.the-clayman.co.uk

Commercial Clay Ltd
Sandbach Road, Cobridge,
Stoke-on-Trent, ST6 2DR
Tel: 01782 274448

Corby Kilns Ltd
Dale St, Corby
Northants, NN17 2BQ
Tel: 01536 269229
Email: info@corbykilns.co.uk
www.corbykilns.co.uk

Cromartie Ltd
Park Hall road, Longton,
Stoke-on-Trent,
Staffs, ST3 5AY
Tel: 01782 319435 / 313947
Fax: 01782 599723
Email: enquiries@cromartie.
co.uk
www.cromartie.co.uk

CTM Supplies
9 Spruce Close, Exeter, EX4 9JU
Tel: 01395 233077
Fax: 01395 233905
E-mail:
CTMSupplies@hemscott.net
www.ctmsupplies.co.uk

Potclays Ltd
Brick Kiln Lane, Etruria,
Stoke- on-Trent, Staffs ST4 7BP
Tel: 01782 219816
Fax: 01782 286506
Email: sales@potclays.co.uk
www.potclays.co.uk

Potterycrafts Ltd
Campbell Road, Stoke-on-Trent,
Staffs, ST4 4ET
Tel: 01782 745000
Fax: 01782 746000
Email:
admin@potterycrafts.co.uk
www.potterycrafts.co.uk

Scarva Pottery Supplies
Unit 20, Scarva Industrial
Estate, Banbridge,
N Ireland, BT32 3QD
Tel: 02840 669699
Fax: 02840 669700
www.scarvapottery.com

Spencroft Ceramics
Spencroft Road,
Holditch Industrial Estate,
Newcastle-under-Lyme,
Staffs, ST5 9JB
Tel: 01782 627004
Fax: 01782 711395

The Potters Connection Ltd
Chadwick St, Longton,
Stoke-on-Trent, Staffs. ST3 1PJ
Tel: 01782 598729
Fax: 01782 593054

Email:
sales@pottersconnection.com
www.pottersconnection.com

Top Pot Supplies
Celadon House, 8 Plough Lane,
Newport, Shropshire, TF10 8BS
Tel: 01952 813203
Fax: 01952 810703
Website: www.toppot.co.uk

Valentine Clay Products
The Slip House, 18-20 Chell St,
Hanley, Stoke-on-Trent,
ST1 6BA
Tel: 01782 271200
Fax: 01782 280008
Email:
sales@valentineclays.co.uk
www.valentineclays.co.uk

North American Suppliers

American Art Clay Company
4717 W.16th Street,
Indianapolis, IN 46222,
Tel: (800) 374-1600 / (317)
244-6871
Email: catalog@amaco.com
www.amaco.com

A.R.T Studio Clay Company
9320 Michigan Avenue,
Sturtevant, WI 53177-2435,
Tel: (262) 884-4278
www.artclay.com

Atlantic Pottery Supplies
15 Canal Street, Dartmouth,
B2Y 2WI9, Nova Scotia,
Tel: +1 902 466 6947
Fax: +1 902 469 4027
Email:
APS@atlanticpottery.com
www.atlanticpottery.com

Axner Pottery Supply
490 Kane Ct, PO Box 621484,
Oviedo, FL 32762-1484
Freephone: 800-843-7057/407-
365-2600
Email: axner@axner.com
www.axner.com

Claymaker
1240 North 13th Street,
San Jose, CA 95112
Tel: +1 (408) 295 3352
Fax: +1 (408) 295 8717
Email: info@clay-planet.com
www.claymaker.com

Clay People
112 Ohio Avenue, Unit 1,
CA 94804
Tel: +1 (510) 236 1492
Fax: +1 (510) 236-2777
Email: people@claypeople.net
www.claypeople.net

Continental Clay Company
1101 Stintson Blvd,
N.E. Minneapolis, MN 55413,
Tel (800) 432 CLAY / +1 (612)
331 9332

Laguna Clay Company
14400 Lomitas Avenue,
City of Industry, CA 91746,
Tel: (800) 452-4862 / +1 (626)
330-0631
Fax: +1 (626) 333 7694
www.lagunaclay.com

Leslie Ceramics Supply Company
1212 San Pablo Avenue
Berkeley, CA 94706
Tel: +1 (510) 524 7363
Fax: +1 (510) 524 2387
www.leslieceramics.com

Mile Hi Ceramics
77 Lipan Street, Denver,
Colorado, 80223-1580,
Tel: (303) 825 4570
Email:
MileHi@MileHiCeramics.com
www.MileHiCeramics.com

Tucker's Pottery Supplies Inc.
Unit 7, 15 West Pearce Street,
Richmond Hill, Ontario,
Canada L4B 1H6,
Tel +1 (905) 889 7705
Fax: +1 (905) 889 7707
E-mail:
info@tuckerspottery.com
www.tuckerspottery.com

Glaze Recipes

From Bridget Drakeford

Celadon

Feldspar	2.25 kg
Whiting	350 g
Zinc	170 g
Flint	450 g

(+ 1% iron oxide)

From Fong Choo

Dirty Snow, cone 04 (1060°C/1940°F)

Frit 3134	25
Nepheline syenite	25
Barium carbonate	5
Zinc oxide	20
Flint	11
Edgar plastic kaolin	10
Titanium dioxide	8

Fong Choo's orange glaze is Spectrum Glazes No. 1166 Bright Orange (cone 4/6, 1160°C–1222°C/2120°F–2232°F)

From David Leach

David Leach – Y'Ching glaze

Cornish stone	25
Whiting	25
China clay	25
Flint or Quartz	25
Red iron oxide	0.5

Joining slip/paste

(From CPA's Clay and Glazes)

(See under Jeremy Nichols.)

From Jeremy Nichols

Ian Pirie's joining slip/paste

The following process is used extensively in industry to create a virtually liquid glue for joining clay together. In many cases, such as joining handles and spouts, there is no need to score the adjoining surface first.

Dry clay body	100
Feldspar	20
Bentonite	20
Gum arabic	20

The dry ingredients are mixed together, dispersing the bentonite. Next, 500 cc water and 5cc Dispex are mixed and added slowly to the dry ingredients, stirring all the time to make a slop. When ready for use, the deflocculated slip *must* be reflocculated by adding a small amount of magnesium sulphate in solution.

From John Leach

Glaze recipe

Potash feldspar	33
China clay	10
Quartz	21
Wollastonite	26
Talc	3
Bentonite	2
HSM ball clay	5

From Kevin de Choisy

Liner glaze

Lead sesquisilicate	80
Hyplas 71	20
(low iron, high ball clay)	

All coloured decorating glazes are based on this with additions of:

Aubergine:	cobalt oxide and manganese dioxide
Eau de Nil:	cobalt oxide and nickel oxide
Green:	copper oxide
Crocus Orange:	synthetic red iron oxide

From Malcolm Davis

Malcolm Davis' carbon trap shino-type glaze

Nepheline syenite	4500 g
Kaolin	2000 g
Soda ash	1900 g
Ball clay	1520 g
Soda feldspar	1080 g
Cedar Heights Redart	600 g

From Meira Mathison

Meira's Blue Matt

Cone 10 (1305°C/2381°F)
(Semi opaque – buttery surface.)

Custer feldspar	1000
Whiting	375
Barium carbonate	350
EPK	350
Gerstley Borate	175
Titanium dioxide	375
Zinc oxide	13
Lithium carbonate	50
Cobalt carbonate	10
Rutile	5

Meira's Spotted Black

Cone 10 (1305°C/2381°F)
(Shiny – use as an overspray.)

Custer feldspar	66
Whiting	5
Silica	12
Yellow iron oxide	17

Meira's Black/Brown

Whiting	66
Zinc oxide	8.7
Custer feldspar	194
EPK	41
Silica	90
Red iron oxide	50

Meira's Copper Blue

Silica	10
Nepheline syenite	50
Spodumene	10
Barium carbonate	30
Copper carbonate	4

Meira's Yellow Matt

Cone 10 (1305°C/2381°F)
(Semi opaque – buttery surface.)

Custer feldspar	1000
Whiting	375
Barium carbonate	350
EPK	350
Gerstley borate	175
Titanium dioxide	375
Zinc oxide	13
Lithium carbonate	50
Yellow iron oxide	50

From Mel Jacobson

Sung style (originally from Nigel Wood)

Talc	3
Wollastonite	27
Feldspar	25
Ball clay	12.5
Kaolin	12.5
Flint	20

Mel's orange glaze

Whiting	22
Feldspar	60
EPK kaolin	18
Zinc oxide	7
Red Iron oxide	6
Rutile	11

From Phil Rogers

Standard ash glaze
1280°C (2336°F) reduction

Any ash	53
Cornish stone	14.5
Potash feldspar	14.5
China clay	6.5
Whiting	4.5
Quartz	7

NB: the last three ingredients may need to be amended, depending on the ash.

Orange slip

Blue ball clay (WBB)	50
China clay	50
Feldspar	50

From Peter Dick

Green slip

Ball clay (HVAR)	100
Copper carbonate	3.5–7.5

Blue slip

Ball clay (HVAR)	100
Cobalt carbonate	1–2.5

Transparent glaze

Lead bisilicate	75.4
Cornish stone	8.0
Whiting	3.0
Quartz	1.3
China clay	5.0
Ball clay (HVAR)	5.0
Bentonite	2.3

From Terry Bell-Hughes

Matt ash

Ash (mixed)	2
Feldspar	2
China clay	1

Fluid ash

Ash (mixed)	3
Feldspar	2
China clay	1

To these a variety of oxides (up to 20% iron/up to 5% copper oxide/up to 10% black stain) can be added to give a palette of colours and textures and used as underglaze colour. Sometimes he makes the fluid ash even more fluid by adding 10% barium carbonate.

Olive ash glaze

Potash feldspar	4 lb
Mixed ash	3 lb
Red clay	1 lb
Whiting	7 oz

Tenmoku type glaze

Potash feldspar	3 lb
Flint	2 lb
Whiting	1 lb
China clay	6 oz
Red iron oxide	10 oz

Chun type glaze

Potash feldspar	3 lb 48
Flint	2 lb 32
Whiting	1 lb 16
Bone ash	4oz 6

From Warren MacKenzie

Grey matt glaze (1320°C/2408°F)

Spar	5
Whiting	3
Kaolin (EPK)	3

From West Marshall

Glaze recipe

Potash feldspar	33
China clay	10
Quartz	21
Wollastonite	26
Talc	3
Bentonite	2
HSM ball clay	5

From Will Levi Marshall

Caramel yellow glaze Cone 9/10 (1280–1305°C/2336–2381°F) reduction or oxidation.
(Gives semi-gloss opaque yellow/tan.)

Petalite	46.0
Nepheline syenite	36.0
Titanium dioxide	12.0
Dolomite	9.0
Grolleg	9.0

High CaO calcium oxide web glaze. Cone 9/10 (1280–1305°C/2336–2381°F).
(Gives a glossy transparent blue.)

Potash spar	15.00
Dolomite	9.00
Barium carbonate	9.00
Whiting	30.00
Ball clay	18.00
Flint	19.00
Bentonite	2.00
Cobalt carbonate	0.50
Red iron oxide	2.00

NB: Barium carbonate is highly toxic – avoid ingestion. Do not use in glazes intended for use with food.

Index